SPECIAL NEEDS:
BRIDGING THE CURRICULUM GAP

Jonathan Solity

and

Shirley Bull

Open University Press

Milton Keynes · Philadelphia

Open University Press
12 Cofferidge Close
Stony Stratford
Milton Keynes MK11 1BY, England
and
1900 Frost Road, Suite 101
Bristol, PA 19007, USA

First Published 1987. Reprinted 1989

British Library Cataloguing in Publication Data
Solity, Jonathan
  Special needs: bridging the curriculum gap.
  1. Learning disabilities
I. Title   II. Bull, Shirley
371.9′043   C4704
ISBN 0-335-10282-4
ISBN 0-335-10281-6 Pbk

Library of Congress Cataloging in Publication Data
Solity, Jonathan.
Special needs: bridging the curriculum gap.
  1. Learning disabled children — Education —
  Great Britain — Curricula.
  2. Curriculum based assessments — Great Britain.
  I. Bull, Shirley   II. Title.
LC4706.G7S64 1987   371.9   87-7652
ISBN 0-335-10282-4
ISBN 0-335-10281-6 (Pbk)

Phototypeset by Dobbie Typesetting Service, Plymouth, Devon
Printed in Great Britain by
St Edmundsbury Press Limited, Bury St Edmunds, Suffolk

SPECIAL NEEDS:
BRIDGING THE CURRICULUM GAP

PREFACE

In recent years, in the United Kingdom, there has been a growing interest in the application of behavioural psychology to the practice of education. This has been reflected in an expanding literature which has described the management of children's behaviour and discussed the development of behavioural approaches to children's learning.

Many accounts of behavioural psychology in education have been formulated and expressed within the context of 'children with special needs'. Behavioural psychology has been seen to embody principles, and a powerful set of techniques, which have been instrumental in enabling teachers and parents to meet children's educational needs and overcome their difficulties.

Three approaches, Task Analysis, Direct Instruction and Precision Teaching, have been the subject of increasing attention by teachers, advisors, lecturers and educational psychologists, in relation to helping children with learning difficulties in mainstream education. Various authors have described the principles and classroom implementation of each approach which has required those working in the field to become familiar with a new vocabulary and set of concepts.

The books and articles published have usually only focused on one of the three approaches and invariably not made detailed reference or comparisons to the other two. This has naturally led to Task Analysis, Direct Instruction and Precision Teaching, being seen in isolation, frequently as three separate, unrelated and interchangeable orientations to teaching. It has therefore not always been easy to see exactly how they link together and contribute to a systematic model for teaching children with special needs. They are, however, highly compatible and complementary. They share similar assumptions and principles, derived from behavioural psychology, which make specific and original contributions to the teaching process.

The purpose of this book is to describe the aims, assumptions, principles and techniques of Task Analysis, Direct Instruction and Precision Teaching and illustrate how they interrelate. Furthermore, they will be placed within the specific context of Curriculum Based Assessment, which emphasises how to identify and make appropriate provision for children's educational needs. Behavioural psychology in general, and the three approaches in particular, convey a feeling of optimism about children experiencing difficulties. They are teacher-centred and focus on factors, affecting how children learn, which are within the teacher's sphere of influence in the classroom. Task Analysis, Direct Instruction and Precision Teaching give the classroom practitioner clear guidelines about how to meet children's needs and emphasise that students can, and will, learn if the teaching is right.

The book has been divided into five parts. *Part I*, First Principles, introduces the principles behind the major theoretical orientations presented. *Chapter 1* provides a brief description of the behavioural model: its assumptions and concepts, together with its specific relevance in teaching children with special needs. The principles on which Task Analysis, Direct Instruction and Precision Teaching are based are then introduced in *Chapters 2, 3 and 4* respectively. *Chapter 5* presents the rationale for Curriculum Based Assessment and explains how the three approaches link together and interrelate and enable children's educational needs to be identified and met. Many of the concepts and themes introduced in *Part I* are then developed and discussed, in more depth, in *Parts II–IV* which focus on the separate steps in the assessment procedure.

Part II concentrates on curriculum design. *Chapter 6* shows how the principles of Task Analysis are incorporated into a model of curriculum development. *Chapter 7* presents a six-step procedure for preparing curricula based on the application of Direct Instruction principles. *Chapter 8*, the concluding one in *Part II*, considers how existing curricula, especially when they are based on published materials, can be adapted and amended according to the guidelines offered by Task Analysis and Direct Instruction.

Part III focuses on how children are placed on the curriculum and how teaching procedures are selected. *Chapter 9* looks at the issues involved, when finding out what children have already learned, so that what they are taught is at the right level of difficulty. *Chapter 10* then describes how the choice of teaching methods is determined by a child's stage of learning each new skill.

Part IV looks at how children's educational progress is evaluated and in so doing discusses, in some depth, the practical applications of Precision Teaching. *Chapters 11, 12 and 13* describe the various steps involved in gathering details about children's progress, whereas *Chapter 14* concentrates on how to make sense of the information that is collated. *Chapter 15* then considers how changes can be made in a teaching programme, should a child's progress not meet our expectations.

Finally, *Part V* has just one chapter, *Chapter 16*, which provides an overview of the book's content and stresses the ways Task Analysis, Direct Instruction and Precision Teaching interrelate and make their specific contributions to the process of Curriculum Based Assessment.

Special Needs: Bridging The Curriculum Gap is written for those seeking guidance on how to increase their effectiveness in the classroom, whether they be students in training or fully qualified teachers. However, we hope the book will also be of assistance to those in related professions, who wish to become more familiar with behavioural psychology, the teaching approaches and assessment procedures based on its principles, and their application to teaching children with special needs.

Authors' Note

In examples which are based on real life situations, names have been altered to protect the anonymity of those concerned. Throughout this book male and female titles and names, and the words she and he are used randomly. In referring to both teachers and children 'she' and 'he' may be interchanged, throughout.

Acknowledgements

There are several groups of people we would like to thank for their time, help, insights and advice during the preparation of this book: Hugh Clench, Margaret Heritage, Mark Solity and Dave Tweddle for their comments and suggestions on draft copies of the manuscript, and Nick Fenwick for helping to proof read the final manuscript. We are indebted to Lyn Beddowes for her faultless typing of the various draft manuscripts and the final manuscript. In particular we would like to express our thanks to Ted Raybould for his encouragement and advice, his attention to detail and stimulating discussion about a number of conceptual issues. We found his help invaluable in preparing the final manuscript. However, responsibility for the views expressed and for any errors and omissions remain, of course, entirely our own. Finally, and most important of all, our thanks to Marian, Harry and our families for their encouragement, support and patience while the book was being written.

CONTENTS

PART III
Deciding What To Teach and How To Teach

PART IV
Looking at Children's Progress

PART I
First Principles

1 LEARNING AND TEACHING: A BEHAVIOURAL VIEW

OVERVIEW

This chapter describes:
— the assumptions behind the behavioural model

— the behavioural model

— how the behavioural model can help in teaching children with special needs

---

To begin thinking about planning classroom practice we need a framework: an overall perspective which gives us both a starting point and a sense of direction. The behavioural model takes a view of the teaching process which is clear and practical and, perhaps most important of all, positive in its philosophy. It provides teachers with a systematic way of describing and interpreting the classroom environment. It directs attention to key questions within the field of education, relating to how children learn and how teachers can maximise their effectiveness in the classroom, when planning to teach children who are experiencing learning difficulties.

There are several key concepts and assumptions associated with the behavioural model (Table 1.1) which encapsulate a powerful and optimistic framework within which to work. They set the scene for teachers and children

Table 1.1 Key Concepts and Assumptions Associated with the Behavioural Model.

Behaviour is learned
Focus on the observable
Learning means changing behaviour
There is no teaching without learning
Our behaviour is governed by the setting in which it occurs (known as setting events) and by what follows our actions (known as consequences)

to experience a positive and successful learning environment. The first part of this opening chapter introduces these concepts and assumptions. We then take a general look at the way teachers and children influence each other's behaviour in the educational and social settings they share, before directing our attention to how the behavioural model can help us to teach children with learning difficulties.

BEHAVIOUR IS LEARNED

The behavioural model focuses on the relationship between behaviour and environment. Its principle tenet is that behaviour is learned and that what we learn and the ways in which we behave, depend on our everyday experiences and the environment in which we live.

In the course of a single day children encounter many different settings. They spend time in school, in their own homes and those of friends, they go to clubs, discos and the cinema and may occasionally go to football grounds and other sporting venues. The children learn certain behaviour patterns from each of these environments and, as a teacher, you cannot affect what they learn from all of them. However, in so far as you determine what happens within your classroom you can, and do, influence the environmental factors from which children learn. Indeed your classroom is, in a sense, an artificial one which is especially designed to teach children a wide range of educational skills and information. Your major role as teacher is to organise it in a way which results in successful learning experiences for the children.

FOCUS ON THE OBSERVABLE

We are all well practiced at interpreting the actions of others, treating the way they behave as an outward indication of what they think and how they feel, as expressions of their attitudes and values. When we say that someone is 'upset', 'excited' or 'irritable', we are making suppositions about how they feel from our observations of their behaviour. Similarly, a teacher may say that a pupil 'lacks confidence', 'is lazy' or 'enjoys reading'. Again, these comments express the teacher's interpretations of her pupil's behaviour, rather than describe what the child actually does.

Since our interpretations about other people's behaviour are essentially personal, they are likely to be coloured by our own expectations and values. Thus, two teachers may react differently to the same behaviour by a pupil, depending on the way they see it and on their expectations. One may read a child's smile when reprimanded as 'insolent'; another may suppose that it is a 'nervous' smile or a sign of embarrassment. These different personal views may result in quite dissimilar ways of handling the same situation.

Moreover, the influence which teacher expectations can have on pupil performance is well documented (for example, Rosenthal and Jacobson, 1968; Barker-Lunn, 1970; Pidgeon, 1970).

Subjective interpretations of behaviour also tend to be vague and open to problems of miscommunication. Take, for example, the blanket terms 'disruptive' or 'aggressive', which a teacher may use to describe a child's behaviour in class. The assumption is that these words mean the same to everybody. However, a number of different behaviours could be covered by the term 'disruptive'. Does the teacher mean the child was humming, talking out of turn, throwing paper darts, knocking over chairs or, perhaps, some other activity? He may mean that the child behaved in one way on Monday and in a different way on Tuesday. The picture of events held by the teacher may therefore look quite different from the point of view of the colleague or parent to whom he is talking.

The assumptions we make when using such general terms can equally lead to miscommunication between teacher and pupils about the ways they should behave. If a teacher tells her pupils to 'Stop messing about' or 'Settle down', she assumes that her pupils share her understanding as to what exactly she means. But do they? These expressions are ambiguous and at least some of her pupils may fail to comply simply because they are uncertain about what their teacher wants them to do.

So it is important for pupils that we try, as far as possible, to take a more objective view of their behaviour in the classroom. The behavioural model and its concern with the *observable* can help us to make sure that our own reactions to events, and our communications of these to others, are as accurate as possible. The model directs us to deal only with those events and actions which can be seen and heard and are measurable. We therefore focus on what the children *do*, rather than how we interpret their behaviour. Examples of non-behavioural descriptions and some possible behavioural alternatives are shown in Table 1.2.

Confining yourself to the observable may initially seem unfamiliar and certainly requires practice, in order to minimise the effects of subjective interpretations and judgements on the way you deal with children's behaviour. However, the advantages of taking this view are many. You will avoid the trap of labelling children. You will see events within the classroom environment more clearly and will increase the clarity of your communication to your pupils, their parents and your colleagues.

LEARNING MEANS CHANGING BEHAVIOUR

Within the behavioural model, learning is indicated by a change in children's 'observable' behaviour. Thus, the way we know that children have learned something is because we can see that their behaviour has altered. They may be able to follow a new routine, read new words or complete a new numerical

Table 1.2   Some Non-behavioural and Behavioural Descriptions.

Non-behavioural	Behavioural
A polite child	— Says, 'Please' and 'Thank you' at appropriate times. — Smiles and says 'Hello Miss' when first entering a class. — Raises hand to ask or tell. — Asks permission to leave seat; or borrow a rubber . . . etc.
Concentrates well during story	— Looks at teacher throughout a ten minute story. — Afterwards, correctly answers questions about the story. — After story, writes story in own words.
Has retention problems	— Read all ten flashcards correctly three times on Friday. On Monday, read only five correctly on three occasions. On Tuesday, read only two correctly on three trials.
He's very aggressive today	— Hit three children during break. — Swore at John when he knocked his chair.

operation. In each instance they can, therefore, be seen as having learned, as a result of acquiring a new behaviour.

Changes in behaviour also occur when we no longer perform an activity which we had previously displayed. We might forget how to do something or replace a particular response with one we regard as more suitable and desirable. This happens frequently, for instance in the case of people who give up smoking. They change their behaviour by stopping smoking and so no longer engage in a harmful activity.

THERE IS NO TEACHING WITHOUT LEARNING

The relationship between teaching and learning within the behavioural framework has been brought into sharp focus by Vargas (1977) who wrote 'Teaching is changing behaviour; it is helping others to learn faster or more efficiently than they would on their own' (p.6). The conclusion to be drawn from this statement is that teaching can only be said to have taken place when learning occurs. Teachers, therefore, directly facilitate this change of behaviour; they make learning possible through their interactions with pupils and ensure that children learn quicker than they would if left on their own.

However, it is equally important to note that learning can, and frequently does, occur in the absence of direct teaching. Pupils learn from a variety of sources, both in and out of school, from peers and the events they see going on around them which do not involve the teacher. On many occasions nobody sets out with the clear intention of teaching but the children nevertheless learn. Much of what they learn is a result of their own curiosity and the routes of discovery on which they embark to explore and investigate their own world. So while we support the view that *there is no teaching without learning*, we feel it must be fully recognised and appreciated that there can be learning without teaching.

HOW THE ENVIRONMENT INFLUENCES BEHAVIOUR

According to the behavioural view, the environment operates in two principal ways to govern behaviour. Firstly, it provides the circumstances in which we behave: we never behave in a vacuum but always in the context of particular surroundings and in response to certain events. (Within the framework of the model we confine ourselves to identifiable, *external* events.) Here we shall refer to these contextual surrounding and events collectively as *setting events* (also described as *antecedents* in the literature). Secondly, the environment, including the people within it, provides the *consequences* which follow our behaviour. Instances of a specific behaviour usually have some effect or outcome and these consequences are important in determining how we will behave in future.

Thus we can look at behaviour within the context in which it occurs and the consequences which follow it;

Setting ————————➤ Behaviour ————————➤ Consequences
Events

If we imagine a slow-motion, action-replay of single instances they might look something like the sequence of events illustrated in Table 1.3.

These events having happened, the consequences can act as the setting events for future behaviour. For example, once the room is light you may walk into it, the teacher's question to Mary is the cue for her to speak, etc. Thus our behaviour and the external events surrounding it link together in a continuous chain of interactions.

Table 1.3   Some Examples of Interactions Between Environment and Behaviour.

Setting events	Behaviour	Consequences
1. The room is dark	Flick the light switch 'on'	The room becomes light
2. Teacher asks Paul a question	He says the correct answer	Teacher confirms as correct and praises Paul
3. Lesson after break has started. Teacher is talking to class	Mary walks into class	Teacher turns and frowns at Mary and asks why she is late
4. An inter-school cricket match. Ball bowled to David	David hits ball clear to the boundary	His school supporters cheer; he scores 6 for his team; the captain praises him

Note. Example 1 shows how the behaviour may cause change simply in the physical environment. In Example 2 the consequences are pleasant, but in Example 3 they are less so. Example 4 illustrates the point that a single piece of behaviour may have several outcomes.

This sequence also provides a framework within which to look at how a teacher organises the learning environment. She plans and arranges *setting events* in the classroom in a way which she hopes will promote successful learning. The areas she concentrates on, primarily, are curriculum development, classroom organisation and selection of suitable teaching methods. They are aspects of the environment that come under the teacher's sphere of influence and can be planned in advance to increase the teacher's effectiveness in teaching children who are experiencing learning difficulties.

Descriptions of children's *behaviour* are expressed in terms of what can be seen and observed in the classroom and are a positive statement of what the children should be able to do after they have been taught. Finally, the teaching approaches we describe incorporate recommendations for deciding how to respond to children's behaviour during teaching sessions. These are the *consequences* and detail the type of feedback and rewards that will help keep the children interested and motivated in their work.

CHILDREN WITH LEARNING DIFFICULTIES

Children who experience learning difficulties come to the attention of their teachers in various ways. First of all they will have fallen behind their peers in learning numeracy and literacy skills. In some cases it is possible they will not have made a start at all. Alternatively, other children may have begun to learn to read and write but will not be picking up new skills as quickly as their peers. In either event, a gap in attainment levels exists between these

children and the rest of the pupils in the class. What is often particularly
worrying is that the gap may actually be widening. Many teachers will have
come across children who were behind in learning important educational skills
but during the course of the school year made excellent progress. However,
the children that cause most concern are those who are not responding to
the teaching they receive and are not improving.

This group of children often appear to lack concentration. After receiving
instructions their attention wanders; they may begin to chatter, move out
of their seats and, generally, adopt a series of strategies to avoid doing any
work. They are likely to be the children who the teacher feels need someone
standing over them all the time to make sure they stay on task and keep
concentrating.

Finally, they may also lack motivation and be quite uninterested in any
form of academic work. It will be hard to find anything to capture their
imagination, which could provide a platform for any future activities. In
short, certain children present us with difficulties because they are behind
their peers on the curriculum, are not making satisfactory progress, lack
concentration and have lost interest in work.

How Can the Behavioural Model
Help us to Teach Children
who are Experiencing Learning Difficulties?

Engelmann and Carnine (1982) looked closely at the relationship between
the environment and the learner. They concluded that before any final
statements could be made about the nature of children's learning difficulties,
the educational environment had to be organised in such a way so that nothing
more could have been done to improve the quality of teaching offered. This
meant that given existing knowledge about how to teach, every attempt should
be made to ensure that the most effective patterns of classroom organisation
and teaching approaches are adopted to teach children with difficulties.

Behavioural Psychology with its concern to describe the learning
environment and explain how children learn, is ideally placed to help
formulate principles about how the classroom environment influences the
teaching process and children's learning. To teach effectively we need to focus
on three specific areas;
— how the environment operates to influence learning outcomes,
— how the information taught to children can be organised to ensure
   optimal learning,
— the most effective methods for communicating skills and knowledge
   from teacher to pupils, so that what is learned is remembered over time
   and can be generalised and applied in other educational settings.
Other models of learning and teaching have addressed themselves to these

areas but never quite in the same way as the behavioural model. The behavioural model focuses entirely on factors which determine how children learn *and over which you have some influence*. We will only be describing aspects of effective teaching which you can do something about.

As the model assumes that all behaviour is learned, we are given an optimistic starting point for teaching children with learning difficulties. If there is anything they cannot do it is because they have not been taught the necessary skills. It is felt that what children learn, ultimately, is very much a case of being in the right place at the right time; getting the appropriate help from school and home to meet their specific educational needs. When children fail to learn as expected this may well not have happened and so future planning aims to teach children what they have missed. It is assumed that *the pupil will learn* when the teaching is right.

The behavioural model only concentrates on aspects of teaching and learning which can be seen and observed. We are not therefore tempted into offering explanations for failure which lead to children being given potentially harmful labels (i.e. educationally subnormal, maladjusted). We only focus on the things a child can and cannot do, those aspects of a child's behaviour which are observable and not open to more than one interpretation. We are not trying to find lengthy explanations about why children have not learned in the past, although many reasons could be offered.

Instead the behavioural model takes a pragmatic view. We cannot change what has already happened but through our role as teachers we can influence the future. The model starts from here; it describes what children *can do* and recommends how they should be taught to overcome previous difficulties.

So we feel the behavioural model gives us an optimistic framework within which to teach children who have experienced difficulties. It concentrates on answering the question, 'How can we teach effectively'? rather than pondering for too long on why children have failed to learn in the past. The aim of teaching is to help children bridge the gap in attainment levels that exists with their peers.

In Chapters 2, 3 and 4 we will introduce the principles of three approaches to teaching children with learning difficulties that have their roots in behavioural psychology. Task Analysis, Direct Instruction and Precision Teaching, although developed independently, provide a natural complement to each other. They emphasise slightly different aspects of the teaching process and when taken together give teachers a powerful means of accelerating children's progress. In Chapter 5, the final chapter in Part I, we describe how the three approaches link together and interrelate within an assessment procedure known as Curriculum Based Assessment.

SUMMARY

Behaviour is learned.

The behavioural model focuses on observable behaviour only. It concentrates on what can be seen and does not attempt to interpret children's behaviour.

For learning to occur there must be a change in pupil behaviour.

There is no teaching without learning. *However*, there can be, and frequently is, learning without teaching.

Our behaviour is governed by the setting in which it occurs and the consequences which follow it.

The classroom environment is organised within the sequence;
setting events ⟶ behaviour ⟶ consequences

When teaching children with special needs the behavioural model concentrates on factors over which teachers have some influence.

RECOMMENDED FURTHER READING

Bull, S. L. and Solity, J. E. (1987). *Classroom Management: Principles to Practice.* Croom Helm, London.
Cheeseman, P. L. and Watts, P. E. (1985). *Positive Behaviour Management.* Croom Helm, London.
Fontana, D. (ed) (1984). *Behaviourism and Learning Theory in Education*, British Journal of Educational Psychology Monograph Series No. 1. Scottish Academic Press.
Wheldall, K. and Merrett, F. (1984). *Positive Teaching: The Behavioural Approach.* Unwin Education Books, London.
White, O. R. (1977). Behaviourism in Special Education: An Area for Debate. *In* R. O. Kneedler and S. L. Tarver (eds) *Changing Perspectives in Special Education.* Charles E. Merrill, Ohio.

2 TASK ANALYSIS

```
┌────────────────────────────────────────────────────────┐
│                      OVERVIEW                           │
│                                                        │
│  This chapter describes:                               │
│  — the principles behind Task Analysis                 │
│  — the three steps involved in completing a Task       │
│    Analysis                                            │
│  — why tasks are written in the form of behavioural    │
│    objectives                                          │
└────────────────────────────────────────────────────────┘
```

The emergence of Task Analysis in mainstream education to teach children with special needs, became quite marked in the United Kingdom in the mid 1970s. The feeling expressed by many educationalists was that it was not sufficient to try and identify 'what was wrong' with children through administering a series of normative tests (tests which compare one child's level of performance with those of another). As the value of these tests became increasingly questioned, attention turned to the curriculum as the starting point for trying to help children experiencing difficulties. It was felt that if the tasks children were to be taught could be broken down into small, carefully sequenced steps, they would make much better progress. The process of identifying these small steps is known as Task Analysis.

In recent years the term 'Task Analysis' has been used in a variety of ways and clear descriptions of what a Task Analysis entails have not been easy to find. The phrase has been interpreted by some to be a means of analysing the precise nature of a task and the skills a pupil will need to be taught in order to learn that task: it describes an end point, what must be learned, but not the methods that will be adopted for teaching.

Others, notably in the field of mental handicap, have assumed a much more expansive role for the process, which describes not only the tasks to be taught, but an analysis of the most appropriate teaching methods for different types of tasks, together with the form in which records should be kept. The description of Task Analysis which follows has more in common with the former approach than the latter and will be concerned with trying to analyse the essential parts of a task. Selection of teaching methods and record-keeping systems will be considered separately in Chapters 10–13.

The model of Task Analysis we describe has three steps which are shown in Table 2.1. The steps describe how a task, once defined, can be broken down

Table 2.1   Steps Involved in a Task Analysis.

Step 1	Describe the task
Step 2	Isolate, sequence and describe all the essential skills connected with the task
Step 3	Slice tasks and skills

into a series of component skills which are sequenced in order of difficulty. Teaching earlier skills facilitates learning later skills in the sequence.

STEP 1. DESCRIBE THE TASK

Howell *et al.* (1979) have suggested that the first step in describing the process of task analysis is to be able to identify and define *a task*. However, the term a 'task' is ambiguous and can be used to refer to a variety of activities which children can undertake during the school day. They can be set tasks in relation to learning to read and write but tasks can also be set in connection with social behaviour. They may be asked to complete a piece of work, hand out a set of books to their classmates or collect art materials from a stock room. Many other examples of tasks could be generated, all of which are a necessary part of everyday school life. As the topic of the book is helping children with learning difficulties, we want to confine the discussion to identifying tasks which children have to complete in order to learn reading, writing and numeracy skills. We have adopted Howell *et al.*'s (1979) definition of a task as being 'any behaviour or set of behaviours that a child must engage in to demonstrate the acquisition of skill or knowledge' (p. 80).

The proposal is that children have to perform an activity which can be observed, in order to satisfy a teacher that a skill has been learned. Mager (1962) and Gronlund (1970) have both written lucid accounts of how children's academic tasks can be formulated in such terms. Mager has argued that an important reason for requesting children to perform an *observable act* which shows the task has been learned, is so there can be no doubt amongst the teachers coming into contact with the children, that the task has been mastered. This has particular relevance for those children experiencing difficulties. We must be sure that children have learned the tasks we set out to teach. We would not want to transfer them to a new activity before they were absolutely ready. For example, let us suppose we wish to teach a pupil to read a group of consonant, vowel, consonant (CVC) words. Consider the following descriptions of this task

Description 1 —   Pupil knows how to read CVC words.
Description 2 —   Pupil reads a list of 20 CVC words orally with 100% accuracy.

Which description would leave you with least doubt about whether the task has been performed satisfactorily? Think of the range of activities which are subsumed under the verb 'to know'. Does this term require the child to read CVC words orally, write CVC words from dictation, underline the CVC words in a reading book, etc? All these activities could be taken as being within the range of competence of a pupil who knew how to read CVC words. However, unless the pupil's task is described by a verb which indicates an observable behaviour, doubts and ambiguities will exist about precisely what the pupil has to do to show that he knows how to read CVC words.

Table 2.2 lists a group of verbs which are open to many interpretations when it comes to deciding whether the child can perform the task.

Table 2.2 Non-observable Verbs.

to know
to understand
to appreciate
to acknowledge
to enjoy

What behaviour is expected from a pupil who knows, understands, appreciates, etc? They are verbs which do not indicate a clear, unambiguous act, that can be completed to demonstrate that a skill or concept has been learned. If a pupil approaches you and claims she knows all the monarchs who have ruled England since 1066, you would probably consult a history book and ask appropriate questions to check out the pupil's claim. The pupil would need to answer questions, probably orally or in writing and therefore act in a way that was consistent with her assertion.

The terms we prefer to adopt for describing how children complete tasks are listed in Table 2.3.

They are more useful terms for describing tasks since they are all verbs which indicate observable behaviour. Furthermore, when performed, each has a distinct beginning and end, meaning it can also be *counted*. For example, when a pupil writes a word, or draws a line it is clear when each task is started

Table 2.3 Appropriate Verbs for Describing Children's Behaviour.

to write
to read orally
to underline
to draw
to trace
to copy
to point
to touch

and finished. Being able to count the frequency of occurrence of a particular academic behaviour is, as we shall see later, extremely important.

STEP 2. ANALYSE THE TASK

The second step in the process of Task Analysis is to identify other skills that a pupil must be taught in order to perform the task you wish to teach. This involves isolating, sequencing and describing all of the essential skills connected with that task.

Many of the tasks thus identified for children to learn involve them in using a range of skills, either in isolation or in combination in a pre-determined sequence. Think of the skills required to teach a pupil to tie her shoe-laces, write her name from memory, catch a ball, locate a word in a dictionary, etc. When writing her name from memory the pupil would have to hold a pencil appropriately, form individual letters and sequence those letters correctly. Each skill is essential to the task and a failure to learn one or more of them, would mean that mastering the task of which they form a part would be extremely difficult—if not impossible.

Much of what is taught in schools can be thought of as a series of tasks which involve the use of a set of related skills. Successful teaching will depend, in part, upon the extent to which teachers are able to isolate, sequence and describe the essential skills of the tasks being taught.

Let us imagine we wish to teach a task, which we will call Task A. The analysis starts when we ask the question 'What skills does the child need to have been taught in order to perform Task A?' The skills can then be identified and arranged in order of difficulty.

e.g.

$$\boxed{\text{Task A}}$$
$$\uparrow$$
Skill 4
$$\uparrow$$
Skill 3
$$\uparrow$$
Skill 2
$$\uparrow$$
Skill 1

Each skill reflects a different, but essential, activity that the pupil needs to perform to complete Task A. Skill 1 is the easiest of the four skills and is therefore taught first. It is followed, in order of increasing difficulty, by skills 2, 3 and 4. Teaching the earlier, and usually easier skills, will facilitate the pupil's learning of the later, and possibly more difficult skills. Furthermore, if a pupil can perform skill 4, the most difficult of the four skills, it can be assumed the pupil can also complete the earlier and easier skills (skills 1, 2 and 3).

We can illustrate this process further if we consider the task analysis which results from a common task in many infant classrooms, teaching children to name the colours of a group of objects. Here five different colours are represented: yellow, black, red, green and blue.

Our analysis starts by asking the question, 'What skills does a pupil need to be taught to name colours'? Each skill subsequently isolated, involves an activity which is different from that needed to perform other identified skills. One possible task analysis for the example given is shown in Table 2.4

In this sequence each skill makes different demands on the pupil. Children progress from matching to sorting, to a recognition activity and then, finally, to naming colours. Teaching pupils the earlier and easier skills facilitates their acquisition of the later and relatively more difficult ones. This step can be contrasted with the third step in task analysis known as slicing.

Table 2.4 An Example of a Task Analysis.

Task —
> *Names* colours when shown an object and asked
> 'What colour is this?'

↑

Skill 3 — *Recognises* colours, i.e. answering 'yes' or 'no' when asked, 'Is this colour red?' or pointing to the appropriate coloured object when asked 'Show me a _____ one'.

↑

Skill 2 — *Sorts* objects according to their colour.

↑

Skill 1 — *Matches* colours to a model.

STEP 3. SLICING TASKS AND SKILLS

Here a given task or skill is made easier for the pupil without, however, altering the nature of that task or skill. The demands of the task or skill are reduced but in a manner which enables their essential features to remain the same. For example, the above task and three skills can be made easier and still involve the pupil in the same activity. Let us consider the first and easiest skill in the sequence, matching colours.

A child would be required to match objects to their respective models on the basis of colour. Yellow objects would be selected and placed next to the yellow model; black objects would be selected and placed next to the black model; red, green and blue objects would also be selected and placed next to the appropriate models. The skill can be made easier by reducing the number of colours to be matched from five to two, for example only yellow and black. The child would therefore be presented with objects coloured yellow and black together with yellow and black models for them to be matched against. When the pupil can complete this successfully a third colour may be introduced, thus necessitating that three different colours be matched to their respective models. Gradually the number of colours to be matched would be increased to the original five.

In each of these examples the pupil's activity has remained the same — matching colours. All that has changed is the actual number of colours to be matched, the original five being reduced to two and then being slowly increased. Eventually the pupil is expected to match five colours again but only after two, three and four colours have been matched. A similar process of slicing could occur when teaching sorting, recognising and naming.

WRITE TASKS, SKILLS AND SLICES
AS BEHAVIOURAL OBJECTIVES

So far we have referred to the need to describe tasks, skills and slices in terms of an activity which can be observed. However, before they can be expressed with complete clarity and be free from ambiguity, two additional areas need to be considered. The first relates to the conditions under which the activity is performed. The second defines how well the activity must be completed before it can be said it has been truly learned by the pupil.

The conditions outline the materials to be used when completing the activity and how they are to be presented to the pupil. This will be in one of two ways; visual or oral. Children can be given tasks within a visual format, for example, reading from a book, completing sums presented on a page of paper etc., or, alternatively, a task can be presented orally, as in spelling or mental arithmetic. The conditions provide the setting in which the pupil's task is to be completed and ensure it is presented in the same way each time it is given.

Deciding on an acceptable level of performance to indicate that learning has occurred is problematic because there is little published research available to guide teachers in this matter. Yet it is a highly important area, since we would not want children experiencing difficulties to move on to a new task before we were sure they had mastered their present one. Establishing criteria for success will be considered in detail in our discussions on Precision Teaching. For the time being it is important to remember that all activities should include criteria for successful performance. The tasks, skills and slices children learn should therefore make reference to three areas:
— a clear description of what the pupil must do, expressed as a verb, so that it can be observed,
— the conditions under which the activity will be performed,
— criteria for successful performance.
Descriptions of tasks, skills and slices stated in this way are known as

behavioural objectives. Their use in special education has been advocated widely in recent years and, when used wisely, they can enhance a teacher's effectiveness when teaching children with special needs.

We can therefore look at the process of Task Analysis as follows. Academic skills that we wish to teach need to be expressed in the form of an observable verb, indicating a task that a child must complete, to demonstrate that learning has taken place. However, this task may well be too difficult and can be made easier by identifying its component skills which are also described as observable activities. The third step in the process is slicing where either our original task, or its component skills, can be made easier by reducing the number of examples presented to children. Finally, tasks, skills and the activities that result from slicing are all expressed in the form of behavioural objectives.

SUMMARY

The process of Task Analysis has three steps;
— describing the task,
— identifying components skills,
— slicing tasks and skills.

All the above are expressed in the form of behavioural objectives.

A behavioural objective describes;
— what the pupil must do in observable terms,
— the conditions under which activities are performed,
— criteria for successful performance.

RECOMMENDED FURTHER READING

Ainscow, M. and Tweddle, D. A. (1984). *Early Learning Skills Analysis*. John Wiley, Chichester.

Ainscow, M. and Tweddle, D. A. (1979). *Preventing Classroom Failure: An Objectives Approach*. John Wiley, Chichester.

Gardner, J. G. and Tweddle, D. A. (1979). Some Guidelines for Sequencing Objectives. *Journal of the Association of Educational Psychologists*, **5**, 2, 23–29.

Hannum, W. (1974). Towards a Framework for Task Analysis. *Educational Technology*, **14**, 2, 57–58.

Leach, D. J. and Raybould, E. C. (1977). *Learning and Behaviour Difficulties in School*. Open Books, London.

Lewis, J. M. (1981). Answers to 20 Questions on Behavioural Objectives. *Educational Technology*, **21**, 3, 27–31.

3 DIRECT INSTRUCTION

```
OVERVIEW

This chapter describes:
— the principles behind Direct Instruction

— how children can be taught to generalise

— the assumptions about the learner
```

INTRODUCTION

Direct Instruction originates from Champaign, Illinois, in the USA. It began in the early 1960s when Wes Becker, Carl Bereiter, Siegfried Engelmann and Jean Osborne started working with culturally disadvantaged children. Their initial work focused on teaching language skills and has subsequently been developed to include the teaching of reading, arithmetic and spelling. Their early views on teaching are presented in Bereiter and Engelmann (1966) and emphasise the extent to which teachers can use all the resources available, in the classroom environment, to facilitate significant improvements in children's learning.

Direct Instruction begins by trying to answer the question:

'What is the most effective way to teach children?'

The focus of attention is those classroom variables that are within the teacher's sphere of influence and which determine how effectively children are taught. Direct Instruction therefore sets out to analyse the teaching environment: the curriculum, classroom organisation and teaching procedures, to derive a series of principles on which successful teaching can be based. Direct Instruction is an educational theory which relates to teaching and the process of instruction.

Much educational research and especially that in the area of special needs has attempted to answer the more frequently posed question:

'How do children typically learn?'

In a search for an answer to the question, researchers have concentrated on individual differences between children and looked closely at how they have learned. Research has focused on the children and an analysis of their various characteristics which affect the way they learn. Direct Instruction represents a shift in emphasis from studying the child to conducting a thorough analysis of the teaching process. We wish to stress, however, that in our opinion these two orientations are neither contradictory nor mutually exclusive. To pursue the answer to one question, in preference to the other, emphasises researching and studying one set of variables rather than another, but should not be seen as denying or ignoring the validity of the alternatives.

Children experiencing learning difficulties have less time available to be taught all they need to learn, if the gap in attainment levels that exists between them and their peers is to be narrowed. A child of seven who has not yet started to read has much ground to make up on the other children in her class. She therefore needs to be taught *'more in less time'*, if the standard of her reading is to be the same as other children by the time she is eleven and ready to transfer to her secondary school.

To achieve this aim the teaching offered has to be highly effective. The time spent teaching each day must be organised and planned, in such a way, to help the pupil learn and catch up with her peers. A teacher has to maximise his daily contact time with the pupil so he can be sure that learning is taking place. In Direct Instruction the route to realising these hopes lies in teaching children to *generalise* the skills they have learned. Through the process of generalisation they will be able to apply their skills and knowledge to previously unseen material and in so doing their progress will be accelerated.

When learning literacy and numeracy skills there is a vast amount of information to be acquired. If each piece of information had to be taught separately, it is unlikely there would be sufficient time available to teach everything that needs to be learned. However, the process can be speeded up by showing children how to generalise so they can extend their skills to new areas that they have not previously encountered.

We are, probably, all familiar with a young child's first attempts to generalise. They invariably call all men 'daddy' or all women 'mummy'. On the basis of the child's experience she is usually entirely justified in thinking that all men are called 'daddy'. In time, however, as the child grows older she will realise that the generalisation was not correct and that not all men can be called 'daddy'. She will recognise that only one man can be called 'daddy' and equally only one woman can be called 'mummy'. A similar error occurs when all four-legged animals are called 'dogs'. This happens until children grow older and acquire further information which enables them to distinguish between different categories of four-legged animals.

In normal everyday life, as in the example above, children are regularly checking out their knowledge of the world, testing out boundaries and seeing where generalisations are appropriate or inappropriate. Where children are behind their peers in academic attainment this process of learning to generalise, through trial and error, will in all probability take too long. The children will not make all the necessary connections they need to make if their progress is to be accelerated and if they are to bridge the gap that exists with their peers. The teacher, therefore, has to show the children how to generalise to be absolutely sure that essential skills are learned. The aim therefore, in Direct Instruction, is to organise the curriculum in a way that teaches children skills which can then be generalised.

TEACHING CHILDREN TO GENERALISE

Teaching children to generalise involves looking at the tasks pupils are given which require identical responses. The features of those tasks which are the same then have to be identified, so they can be shown to the children. Imagine taking a child who has acquired the concept of 'a table' into a furniture shop. The range of tables on view is likely to be enormous. How is it then, that despite their differences, all the tables present would be given the same verbal label by the child? They are all objects which she would name 'table', and yet they look so different. The task facing the curriculum designer, therefore, is to identify those features of the various tables which are the same and to devise a teaching programme to communicate those features to the learner. As well as teaching pupils how a range of tables have common characteristics, they must also be shown how they differ from other objects (e.g. a chair or a stool which can also have four legs).

As a result, if children are to be taught to make appropriate generalisations, the presentation of the task must be *consistent with one, and only one*

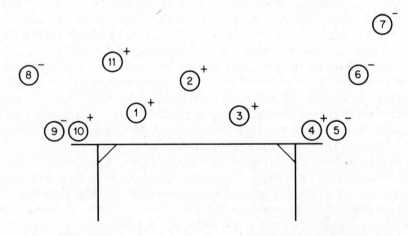

Figure 3.1 Sequence of examples for teaching 'over' and 'not over'.

interpretation. This is achieved by selecting examples, designed to teach a concept, which show how instances of that concept are the same. However, to be sure the child learns to generalise, tasks must also be presented which are *not* examples of the concept being taught and therefore show critical differences.

Deciding how to teach a new concept focuses on presenting examples of what the new concept is, and examples of what the new concept is not. It is only by showing positive and negative examples that a prediction can be made about the range of generalisations that the pupil will be able to make.

We can see how this is achieved by looking at the way the preposition 'over' could be taught. Figure 3.1 shows a sequence of examples for presenting 'over' and 'not over'. Examples 1, 2, 3, 4, 10 and 11 are instances of 'over'. Examples 5, 6, 7, 8 and 9 are instances of 'not over'. The circles indicate the position an object would be held to illustrate 'over' and 'not over'. The numbers represent a sequence for presenting the object in its suggested positions. A range of instances of 'over' and 'not over' are presented so the

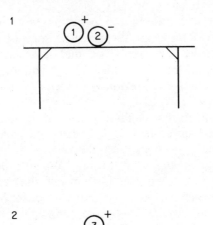

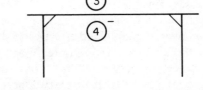

Figure 3.2 Examples illustrating instances of minimal change.
Note:
(a) Presentation 1 is 'over.
(b) Presentation 2 which is 'on' the table is a negative example and is therefore classified as 'not over'.
(c) Presentation 3 is 'over' but presentation 4 is 'under' the table and is also classified as 'not over'.

pupil can see that height above the table is not a significant factor when determining the status of the object. Note how when a change occurs from over to not over (4 to 5) or vice versa (9 to 10), the movement of the object is kept to a minimum so drawing the pupil's attention to the salient features of the concept. Figure 3.2 shows other instances where a minimal change could occur.

1 and 2 demonstrate that when the object is on the table it is classified as 'not over'. Similarly 3 and 4 demonstrate when the object is under the table it is also classified as being 'not over'. By presenting the series of examples in this way the teaching method is consistent with one and only one interpretation.

Finally, we need to mention briefly the assumptions that are made about the learner within the approach. The first is that for children to be taught to generalise they must be able to do two things:
— identify and discriminate any characteristic of the task presented through examples (e.g. colour, shape etc.)
— respond to new examples, on the basis of the identified characteristic when taught to do so.
In the given example, where the concept being taught is 'over', the pupil has to attend carefully to all the examples presented, some of which are labelled 'over' and others labelled 'not over'. The child has to identify the common characteristic of the examples labelled 'over' and then generalise this knowledge to a series of new, previously unseen examples and label them as 'over' and 'not over'.

Secondly it is assumed that children will learn, as long as the teaching is well organised and implemented. It is felt that what they ultimately learn will be entirely consistent with the quality of teaching received. Good teaching results in successful learning. Where children fail to learn in the ways we had hoped, teaching has not met their educational needs. This provides the teacher with an opportunity to reflect on her selection of objectives, choice of teaching methods and patterns of classroom organisation, so the necessary amendments can be made. Within the approach, 'the children are always right': how they respond to our teaching is their way of giving feedback on its overall quality and effectiveness. When they learn they are telling us our teaching was appropriate. When they do not, the message is that it did not meet their needs and has to be altered in some ways.

Direct Instruction encourages us to plan every aspect of our teaching thoroughly and well in advance. By doing this a teacher can place himself in the shoes of the child and look for any lack of clarity or ambiguity in the presentation of new skills. Is the presentation consistent with only one interpretation? Are the instructions straightforward, clear and easy to follow? Is there any aspect of my teaching that could confuse the child?

The importance of Direct Instruction is the emphasis it places on teaching children how to generalise the skills they have learned. This is recognised as being the key feature in enabling children with special needs to bridge the curriculum gap.

SUMMARY

Direct Instruction sets out to answer the question,
   'What is the most effective way to teach children?'

It shows how children's progress can be accelerated so they can be taught more in less time.

Children are taught how to generalise the skills they learn. This is done by showing how examples of a concept are the same. They are also shown how the new concept differs from other concepts they have learned.

Teaching programmes are designed to be consistent with one, and only one, interpretation.

It is assumed that children will learn as long as the teaching is well planned and implemented. What they learn, ultimately, will be entirely consistent with the quality of our teaching.

RECOMMENDED FURTHER READING

Carnine, D. W. (1977). Direct Instruction — DISTAR. *In* N. G. Haring and B. Bateman (eds) *Teaching the Learning Disabled Child*. Prentice Hall, New Jersey.

Carnine, D. W. and Becker, W. (1982). Theory of Instruction: Generalisation Issues. *Educational Psychology*, **2**, 3–4, 249–262.

Engelmann, S. (1980). *Direct Instruction*. Educational Technology Publications Inc., New Jersey.

Engelmann, S. (1980). Towards the Design of Faultless Instruction: The Theoretical Basis for Concept Analysis. *Educational Technology*, **20**, 519–523.

Engelmann, S. and Carnine, D. W. (1982). *Theory of Instruction: Principles and Applications*. Irvington, New York.

4 PRECISION TEACHING

OVERVIEW

This chapter describes:
— the key questions addressed by Precision Teaching when teaching children with special needs
— the assumptions behind Precision Teaching
— the five steps involved in Precision Teaching

Precision Teaching was developed by Ogden Lindsley in the early 1960s at the University of Kansas in America. He had been a student of B. F. Skinner, one of the leading exponents of the behavioural approach. Lindsley looked at how behavioural psychology could be applied to measuring students' academic and social behaviour in the classroom. His work has subsequently provided the basis for much of the research carried out at the Experimental Education Unit at the University of Washington, under the supervision of Norris Haring, Tom Lovitt, Owen White and their colleagues.

Precision Teaching is a precise, systematic approach to teaching. It emphasises the need for carefully structured curricula, provides techniques for collecting detailed information on children's progress and enables the teacher to evaluate the effectiveness of selected teaching procedures. Despite its name, *Precision Teaching is not actually a method of teaching*, rather *it is a way of finding out what teaches*. The techniques of Precision Teaching, when taken on their own, do not contain any information on how to teach. Nowhere do they prescribe that teaching must be conducted in a particular way or that information should be presented to pupils in a certain style. What Precision Teaching does is tell you whether your selected methods have been effective.

Precision Teaching sets out to answer five questions that are frequently asked when teaching basic academic skills to children experiencing learning difficulties.

Are Children Working on the Right Task?

Quite often children do not make the progress for which we had hoped because they are not correctly placed on the curriculum. When this happens, it is most likely that they will be working on tasks which are too hard and for which they have not learned the prerequisite skills. Southgate *et al.* (1981) illustrated how often children are given work which is either too easy or too difficult. In their survey they found that only 30% of the children they looked at were on reading books which were at the appropriate level of difficulty. When teaching children with learning difficulties it helps if they can experience success as quickly as possible. The starting point for future progress is setting children work at the right level of difficulty to meet their educational needs.

Are Children Learning?

Teachers need to know whether pupils are learning and this is especially important when teaching children who are experiencing learning difficulties. It is often said of these pupils that they lack concentration, have a poor memory, cannot retain information from one day to the next, rarely complete set work and require constant attention and supervision. If they can be shown they are making progress, it is to be hoped their motivation will increase and that they will subsequently become more interested in work. Gradually, as they continue to learn and improve, they will see themselves in a more positive light and recognise that they are capable of learning. It is, therefore, important that we can find out whether children are learning from day to day.

Are Children Learning Quickly Enough?

Precision Teaching is not only used to show that children are learning. We need to know whether they are learning quickly enough to catch up with their peers. We can quite rightly feel happy when children who presented difficulties begin to learn, but we must remember there is only a limited amount of time to teach these pupils the skills they need to be taught. Thus Precision Teaching is not just concerned with showing progress, but with demonstrating that pupils' progress is being accelerated, so that they can eventually perform at a level comparable with their peers.

What do I do if Children are not Learning Quickly Enough?

There will be some occasions when you feel children's progress is not satisfactory. Precision Teaching offers a set of systematic strategies, which can be followed, to try and overcome the situation. The aim is to identify teaching procedures which will help teach children so that learning occurs at an optimal rate.

When Can I Move on to the Next Task?

This final question is one of education's 64,000 dollar questions. To our knowledge very little experimental work has been carried out to assist teachers in answering this question. Many teachers will have their own system worked out to help them decide that a skill has been mastered and that the pupil is therefore ready to move on to the next one. Precision Teaching offers guidelines which can provide a common language for determining whether or not skills have been learned. Although there will never be complete agreement on how well a child has to perform on a specific task before it can be said to have been mastered, Precision Teaching makes the entire process overt and open to scrutiny. Precision Teaching has been described, in varying levels of detail, in both American and British educational contexts. Raybould and Solity (1982) have outlined five basic steps (Table 4.1).

Table 4.1   Five Basic Steps in Precision Teaching.

Step 1	Specify children's tasks in observable, measurable terms
Step 2	Record progress on a daily basis
Step 3	Chart progress on a daily basis
Step 4	Record the teaching approach in relation to children's progress
Step 5	Analyse the data to determine whether: — progress is satisfactory or unsatisfactory — changes are needed in teaching approach in order to maintain or accelerate progress

SPECIFY CHILDREN'S TASKS IN OBSERVABLE, MEASURABLE TERMS

As in Task Analysis and Direct Instruction, children's tasks need to be described in terms of an activity that is both observable and measurable. As we will see, it is particularly important that students' performances are described in this way so that the succeeding steps can be completed.

RECORD PROGRESS ON A DAILY BASIS

One of the special features of Precision Teaching is the way daily records are collected. Its special feature can be appreciated by considering the following example. Mary has been given sums to complete over a ten-day period. All were of the same type and level of difficulty. Before reading any further, look at Mary's results in Table 4.2 and decide what interpretations you could draw from her daily records. (Mary did not make any errors over the ten-day period.)

Table 4.2   Mary's Results.

Day	Number of sums correct
Monday	20
Tuesday	30
Wednesday	36
Thursday	40
Friday	60
Monday	32
Tuesday	36
Wednesday	37
Thursday	40
Friday	48

A careful examination of Mary's data suggests that progress was made during the first week, where she improved from 30 correct responses at the beginning of the week to 60 correct responses by the end of the week. However, it appears that forgetting occurred over the weekend because by the second Monday, Mary's performance was down to 32 correct responses. Although steady progress was again made during the second week, Mary did not appear to reach the same high levels achieved during week one.

However, Table 4.3 provides a highly important piece of information which helps to increase the validity of comparisons from one day to the next.

When the time allowed to complete the sums is taken into account Mary's progress can be viewed quite differently. During the first week she was given 20 minutes, but during the second week only 10 minutes were

Table 4.3   Mary's Results (*continued*).

Day	Number of correct sums	Time allowed
Monday	20	20 minutes
Tuesday	30	20 minutes
Wednesday	36	20 minutes
Thursday	40	20 minutes
Friday	60	20 minutes
Monday	32	10 minutes
Tuesday	36	10 minutes
Wednesday	37	10 minutes
Thursday	40	10 minutes
Friday	48	10 minutes

available to complete the sums. Our initial look at the data suggested that Mary improved during the first week but that no further progress was made during the second. However, knowing how much time was available leads to a different conclusion. Thus we see from Table 4.3 progress was, in fact, maintained during the second week also.

The unit of measurement chosen to represent these gains is *rate per minute*. Table 4.4 shows Mary's gains when expressed in terms of the number of correct responses made per minute, on a daily basis.

Table 4.4   Mary's Results (*continued*).

Day	Number of sums correct	Time allowed	Rate per minute
Monday	20	20 minutes	1.0
Tuesday	30	20 minutes	1.5
Wednesday	36	20 minutes	1.8
Thursday	40	20 minutes	2.0
Friday	60	20 minutes	3.0
Monday	32	10 minutes	3.2
Tuesday	36	10 minutes	3.6
Wednesday	37	10 minutes	3.7
Thursday	40	10 minutes	4.0
Friday	48	10 minutes	4.8

In Precision Teaching daily recordings are always timed and children's progress is expressed in terms of the number of *correct responses per minute* and the *number of errors per minute*. In order for these recordings to take place, a daily test has to be prepared to test the specific skill being taught. The daily test is called a *probe*.

An individual probe indicates a pupil's progress on the task being taught. It focuses on a single task and shows how well the pupil is progressing on that specific task. Criteria for success are expressed which demand high levels of both accuracy and fluency, and it is the child's performance in relation to these predetermined standards which are recorded daily.

Probes differ from other 'types of tests' which are typically given in the classroom. The results from a probe do not enable a teacher to make comparisons between a pupil and her peers (normative assessment). Similarly a single probe does not tell you which tasks have been learned in relation to other tasks on the curriculum (criterion-referenced assessment).

Probes have two further important distinguishing features. They are given daily, meaning the teacher gets regular feedback on the effectiveness of her teaching and can take important decisions about the suitability of teaching methods and materials, on the basis of data collected in the classroom. Secondly they take only a short time for the pupil to complete. Most probes last for only one or two minutes, thus, giving the child the opportunity to work at his optimal level without fatigue or boredom setting in.

Probe design depends on the task being taught, but usually involves presenting a large number of examples of the task for the child to complete (in fact more than can be finished in the time available) so his levels of accuracy and fluency can be assessed. This is a topic that we return to, in more detail, in Chapter 11.

CHART PROGRESS ON A DAILY BASIS

Clear and informative feedback can be a major factor in promoting successful learning. Most of you will require few reminders of its effects should you cast your minds back to college days and recollect the air of anticipation prior to a lecturer handing back marked work. It is likely that most people's first response on having work returned, would be to turn to the page containing the grade and comments to see whether their efforts had been appreciated and justly rewarded. Think how you may have felt after working on an essay for many hours only to be awarded a C + and being told you had made a 'good attempt' or something equally uninformative and banal. For most of us when placed in a learning situation, the quality of the feedback we receive will play a large part in determining how successfully we learn. It can help motivate us and sustain interest over a long period of time.

Appropriate feedback is needed by all children but is particularly important for those students who have learning difficulties. They will need to be convinced that they are learning. For many of these children, failing can become a way of life and this makes it all the more difficult to persuade them they are succeeding. Quite often they become desensitised to verbal praise or encouragement and just see it as a ploy by the teacher to get them to work harder. They may shrug off effusive oral praise as just another strategy to get them to sit down and stop messing about.

In Precision Teaching there are three aims in providing feedback:
— to help children appreciate that they are being successful,
— to help motivate them to improve their performance levels,
— to enable them to discriminate between their correct and incorrect responses.

Precision Teaching makes use of charts to provide visual feedback on progress. The charts can make the data obtained from probing more accessible for the child. They have the effect of enabling children to see for themselves just how well they are progressing. This information is equally important to teachers as they will also be in the happy position of seeing how effective their tuition has been.

RECORD THE TEACHING APPROACH

In Precision Teaching we are always trying to find out 'what works best' for children with learning difficulties. We can begin to pinpoint effective teaching approaches by making our teaching systematic and recording how well children learn in response to different patterns of classroom organisation and teaching strategies. This is achieved through keeping a detailed plan of the various key aspects of each lesson, together with any changes that are made from previous lessons and then noting the pupil's subsequent level of performance. Over time the records collected enable teachers to identify which teaching approaches are most effective in promoting children's learning.

ANALYSE THE DATA

Daily inspection of the charts leads to the teacher asking herself the question, 'Is the pupil's progress satisfactory or unsatisfactory'? There are two sources of information which will help answer this question;
— the pupil has, or has not, reached the level set for mastery,
— the pupil's performance on the task is, or is not, improving at a satisfactory rate.
Mastery is the point at which the pupil's level of performance leads us to believe that no further teaching is required on that task. After reaching this level the child could be transferred to a new task. Unfortunately, educational research cannot at this stage offer guidance as to what the mastery level is on any particular task. Therefore the teacher will have to use her experience and professional judgement in deciding whether, or not, mastery has been reached. However, Precision Teaching does provide a number of guidelines to help determine suitable and realistic levels of performance on specific tasks which might be considered to indicate mastery (see Chapter 14).
If the child has not already reached mastery, we are entitled to ask whether the child is improving at a desired rate, in order to reach a specified mastery level. As our aim is to teach as effectively as possible, the teacher needs to set a minimum rate of progress which each pupil has to make, in order to master a new skill. Thus desired rate of improvement in a child's performance over time (daily, weekly, etc.) can be specified in advance by the teacher (e.g. to improve performance levels by 50% on a weekly basis). This can then be represented on a chart, usually by a straight line gradient against which the child's actual rate of progress can be compared. The techniques involved may seem complicated at first, but are relatively easy to learn and help provide a valuable source of information on the pupil's progress, which will enhance the efficiency of teaching.

Many of the ideas associated with Precision Teaching are novel and present an unusual perspective on the teaching process. In particular the notion of quick, timed tests and the use of rate measurement will be unfamiliar to many primary teachers. However, it has a number of advantages. It enables teachers to pinpoint quickly the tasks they are going to teach and ensures that the time spent with children experiencing difficulties, is productive and thoroughly evaluated.

Most children eagerly await the one minute probing so they can see how well they are doing. It is perceived in a totally different light to any other form of 'testing' in which they may have been involved in the past and does not carry any negative overtones. Perhaps most significantly, from the child's point of view, is that she knows exactly what she is supposed to be learning and receives regular feedback on her progress.

SUMMARY

Precision Teaching is not a method of teaching; it is a way of finding out what teaches.

It helps teachers evaluate the effectiveness of their own teaching.

It enables teachers to find out whether children are learning quickly enough to bridge the curriculum gap.

Criteria are provided for successful performance on a task which are based on a child's level of accuracy and fluency.

Children's progress is recorded daily and presented on charts.

The teaching approach is noted and related to children's learning outcomes.

Children's progress is evaluated daily to ensure their learning is being accelerated.

RECOMMENDED FURTHER READING

Alper, T. G. and White, O. R. (1971). Precision Teaching: A Tool for the School Psychologist and the Teacher. *Journal of School Psychology*, **9**, 4, 445–454.

Lovitt, T. C. (1977). *In Spite of my Resistance — I've Learned From Children*. Charles E. Merrill, Ohio.

Neal, D. (1981). The Data-Based Instructional Procedures of Precision Teaching. *Educational Psychology*, **1**, 4, 289–304.

Raybould, E. C. (1981). Precision Teaching: Systematic Instruction for Children with Learning Difficulties. *In* K. Wheldall (ed) *The Behaviourist in the Classroom: Applied Behavioural Analysis in British Educational Contexts*. Educational Review Publications, University of Birmingham.

Raybould, E. C. (1984). Precision Teaching and Pupils with Learning Difficulties — Perspectives, Principles and Practice. *In* D. Fontana (ed) *Behaviourism and Learning Theory in Education*, British Journal of Educational Psychology Monograph Series No. 1, pp. 43–74. Scottish Academic Press.

White, O. R. and Haring, N. G. (1980). *Exceptional Teaching*. Charles E. Merrill, Ohio.

5 CURRICULUM BASED ASSESSMENT

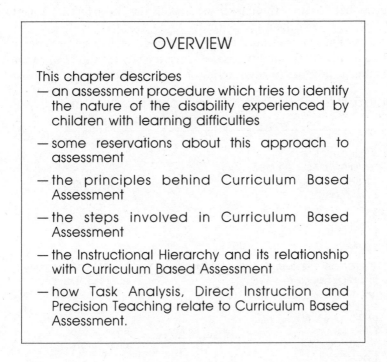

OVERVIEW

This chapter describes
— an assessment procedure which tries to identify the nature of the disability experienced by children with learning difficulties

— some reservations about this approach to assessment

— the principles behind Curriculum Based Assessment

— the steps involved in Curriculum Based Assessment

— the Instructional Hierarchy and its relationship with Curriculum Based Assessment

— how Task Analysis, Direct Instruction and Precision Teaching relate to Curriculum Based Assessment.

In recent years changes in the nature of special education have been reflected in approaches to the assessment process. Tomlinson (1982) traces the ways children have been assessed since the establishment of the early forms of special education in the late eighteenth century. There has been a gradual shift in emphasis from trying to identify a child's handicap to identifying educational needs, irrespective of a pupil's specific disability. This has arisen from the recognition that children's needs often differ, even though they may be suffering from identical handicapping conditions.

Educational needs within this context have been described by Vargas (1977) as, 'behaviours which a person lacks which are necessary in order to function effectively and independently both in the present and in the future' (p. 212). She goes on to say that it is the school's job to identify the skills which will enable individuals to function independently, and to make sure they are learned. Educational needs thus refer to those skills that children must learn to realise the aims we set for their education.

Howell *et al.* (1979) suggest that tests which comprise the process of assessment can be divided into those that classify and categorise pupils, and those that aim to help teachers overcome any problems that children are experiencing. This latter group concentrate on establishing children's educational needs by finding out what skills they have already learned and how best to teach them in the future.

An assessment procedure closely associated with trying to identify the nature of a child's disability has been described by Howell *et al.* (Table 5.1). Assessment involves giving a series of tests, each one designed to find out

Table 5.1   A Sequence for Testing to Identify the Nature of a Pupil's Disability.

Test		Disability
Attainment tests in reading and number	→ pass →	Normal
↓ fail		
IQ	→ fail →	Mentally retarded
↓ pass		
Visual perception (Frostig; Bender Gestalt)	→ fail →	Learning disability (perceptual problem)
↓ pass		
	→ fail →	
Neurological		Brain damaged
↓ pass		
Illinois Test of Psycholinguistic Abilities (ITPA)	→ fail →	Learning disability (processing dysfunction)
↓ pass		
Behaviour checklist	→ fail →	Maladjusted

'what is wrong' with the child. Failure on any particular test leads to the pupil's difficulties being diagnosed and described by the appropriate label. Assessment under these circumstances takes place on a single occasion, frequently outside the classroom. It is divorced from the teaching process and is rarely carried out by the child's own teacher. Instead 'experts' are called in, perhaps an educational psychologist or remedial advisory teacher. This orientation towards assessment has therefore focused on the pupil and tried to identify deficits in aspects of the child's perceptual and cognitive skills which could account for his difficulties.

Ysseldyke and Salvia (1974) have identified four assumptions which underlie this assessment procedure;
— hypothesised 'abilities' can be reliably and validly measured,
— these 'abilities' are causally related to the acquisition of academic skills, and that weaknesses in these areas cause difficulties in learning,
— weaknesses can be corrected or remediated by specially devised training programmes,
— when corrected, the 'strengthened abilities' lead directly to improved performance in basic educational skills.

After examining each assumption in turn, they outlined a number of limitations with this approach towards assessment and felt, 'there was little empirical support for reliable and valid assessment of the hypothesised abilities' (p. 184). They continued, 'there is even less support for programming designed either to "cure" causes or to teach in the light of ability strengths and weaknesses' (p. 184). Ysseldyke and Salvia concluded that the ability training approach clearly fails to meet the assumptions presented above.

Furthermore, such an assessment procedure is not readily endorsed by the more recent trends in special education represented in the Warnock Report (Department of Education and Science, 1978), the 1981 Education Act (DES, 1981) and Circular 1/83 (DES, 1983). Here assessment is viewed as a continuous process taking place over time. It aims to identify children's educational needs and the most appropriate forms of provision to meet those needs.

The alternative approach to assessment (identified by Howell *et al.*) which incorporates this perspective, takes its starting point as the child's classroom. It is the suitability of this environment and the child's interaction with it that is assessed and not the child. The process of assessment which encapsulates these aims is Curriculum Based Assessment (CBA). Elsewhere it has been referred to as assessment-through-teaching (Raybould, 1984; Pearson and Tweddle, 1984). However, the two terms are synonymous and can be used interchangeably.

Curriculum Based Assessment has been defined by Blankenship and Lilly (1981) as, 'the practice of obtaining direct and frequent measures of a student's performance on a series of sequentially arranged objectives derived from the curriculum used in the classroom' (p. 81). As long ago as 1962 Glaser proposed a process to describe this form of assessment which is shown in Table 5.2.

The first stage in the process requires that the curriculum be defined as a series of tasks which are sequenced and expressed in the form of behavioural objectives. Chapter 2 describes how this is done.

Placement on the curriculum, the second stage, identifies which skills have been learned and those which need to be taught in the future. We need to

Table 5.2   Curriculum Based Assessment.

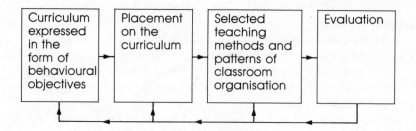

pinpoint exactly where a child is on the curriculum, so that when teaching begins, tasks are set at an appropriate level of difficulty. We do not want to run the risk of giving a child who has experienced learning difficulties work that is too hard. On the contrary these children need to be successful immediately so they can build up their confidence and motivation.

The third stage of the process focuses on the selection of suitable teaching methods, materials and patterns of classroom organisation. This choice is determined by the stage of teaching reached in Haring and Eaton's (1978) Instructional Hierarchy (Table 5.3). The Hierarchy outlines five stages of learning. When children are introduced to a new skill for the first time, they are shown how to perform it accurately.

Table 5.3   The Instructional Hierarchy.

Acquisition	Children are shown how to use a skill for the first time and learn to perform it accurately.
Fluency	Children learn to perform the new skill with fluency as well as accuracy.
Maintenance	Children are still able to perform the skill accurately and fluently even after a period of time when no teaching takes place.
Generalisation	Children are shown how to use the skill in different contexts.
Adaptation	Children are set problems which require them to apply their newly acquired knowledge in novel ways.

Succeeding stages concentrate on developing their use of the skill until they finally reach stage five and are asked to apply their knowledge to real life situations. Haring *et al.* (1981) and White (1981) have researched the Hierarchy in some detail and found that different teaching methods should be used for different stages. The methods used when children are in the acquisition stage are not the most effective ones to adopt when helping children develop fluency. Similarly the methods that enhance fluency are not the most effective in teaching maintenance, generalisation or adaptation. The Instructional Hierarchy and choice of teaching methods for each stage are discussed in some detail, later, in Chapter 10.

In the final stage children's progress is evaluated and related to the selection of teaching methods, patterns of classroom organisation and choice of curriculum. CBA is a process which tries to match these different aspects of teaching input with a child's learning outcomes. The separate parts of the learning environment are within a teacher's immediate sphere of influence and can be altered in the light of what the children learn. Curriculum Based Assessment can therefore be seen as a procedure which sets up situations where links are established between various teaching approaches and pupil progress.

Curriculum Based Assessment provides the context for the classroom application of the behavioural model. Task Analysis, Direct Instruction and Precision Teaching all contribute to different aspects of the process. Task Analysis and Direct Instruction offer the guidelines for helping to prepare the curriculum. Direct Instruction stresses how children can be shown how to generalise the skills they learn when the curriculum is sufficiently well prepared. This is the key to helping them bridge the curriculum gap.

Precision Teaching embodies a series of principles which can assist us in placing children accurately on the curriculum and evaluating their progress in response to carefully planned, systematic instruction. It provides information on the effectiveness of selected teaching methods. The name Precision Teaching can cause confusion at times. When first encountering the approach, the expectation created is that it outlines specific teaching methods for teaching children with special needs. It does not do this. Instead the teacher, relying on her professional training and previous experience, chooses methods which seem to be the most suitable for the child being taught. Precision Teaching gives the teacher feedback on whether these methods were successful. When children learn the teacher knows that the selected methods were effective. If children fail to learn, an alternative teaching approach can be adopted. All the time, the teacher is gathering more information on what does work for some pupils and what does not. As a result her teaching will become more effective as a compendium of successful teaching approaches is compiled.

The following three parts of the book develop each of the steps in CBA. Part II focuses on curriculum design, Part III on placing children on the curriculum and deciding what to teach, and Part IV on evaluation.

SUMMARY

Approaches to assessment which identify the nature of children's handicaps do not readily translate into programmes of remediation.

Curriculum Based Assessment is a four-step procedure which identifies children's educational needs and provides a framework for structured and systematic teaching.

It also provides the context for the classroom application of Task Analysis, Direct Instruction and Precision Teaching.

The aim of teaching is to help children learn skills and concepts which can ultimately be generalised and applied to real life situations.

The Instructional Hierarchy outlines teaching approaches which are most effective for different stages in learning.

RECOMMENDED FURTHER READING

Arter, J. A. and Jenkins, J. R. (1979). Differential Diagnosis — Prescriptive Teaching: A Critical Appraisal. *Review of Educational Research*, **49**, 4, 517–555.

Engelmann, S. (1967). Relationship Between Psychological Theories and the Act of Teaching. *Journal of School Psychology*, **5**, 2, 93–100.

Gillham, B. (1978). The Failure of Psychometrics. *In* B. Gillham (ed) *Reconstructing Educational Psychology*. Croom Helm, London.

Jenkins, J. R. and Pany, D. (1978). Standardised Achievement Tests: How Useful for Special Education? *Exceptional Children*, **44**, 448–453.

PART II
Designing the Curriculum

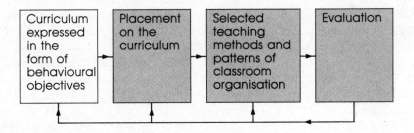

6 TASK ANALYSIS AND CURRICULUM DEVELOPMENT

OVERVIEW

This chapter describes:
— the background to identifying educational aims for children with special needs
— the steps in preparing a curriculum based on the principles of Task Analysis

Part II examines the ways in which the principles of Task Analysis and Direct Instruction are applied to designing a curriculum. Each approach will be discussed in turn, before finally considering how existing curricula can be adapted and amended, according to the guidelines offered by Task Analysis and Direct Instruction.

Most of the principles described are illustrated with examples drawn from reading and arithmetic curricula. Careful thought has gone into the selection of suitable examples, but the very nature of the subject matter means that the examples used are often only one of a number of alternatives. Similarly the skill sequences presented are not put forward as the definitive sequences for teaching reading and arithmetic. There may well be instances when you feel that more appropriate examples could have been selected. On occasions where you consider this to be the case, we would wish you to focus your thoughts and discussions upon the principles by which the curricula are developed, rather than being sidetracked into debating the precise content of our examples. We also recognise that an essential aspect of curriculum development is the need to prepare a thorough record keeping system. This is certainly an important feature of Task Analysis and Direct Instruction. However, in Part II we intend to concentrate on curriculum design only and reserve discussions on record keeping to Part IV.

Let us start by briefly considering some of the factors which may influence how tasks are selected for inclusion in the basic skills curriculum. Most primary teachers are able to articulate the aims they have in relation to what they hope to teach the children in their care. Those aims are likely to encompass moral and social influences as well as the strictly educational. Aims will reflect a school's philosophy of education which will have evolved over a period of time. Teaching staff will have a clear view of what they would like to be able to offer pupils, and have expectations of the qualities they hope children will acquire upon leaving school. This philosophy will represent a variety of factors and influences. It will reflect the attitudes and opinions of staff, both past and present, who have taught in the school. These in turn will reflect attitudes and values prevalent in the society of which they are members.

It is not our intention to discuss at length how schools might attempt to rationalise and formulate their aims of education. Rather we wish to acknowledge their existence, and that the way children are taught will mirror the aims espoused by a particular school. Thus the subject matter chosen will inevitably project the ethos of a school and children's acquisition of specified attitudes, values and skills, will in turn, contribute to those aims being achieved.

In our society it is generally considered desirable that its members should be able to lead independent and fulfilling lives; that they should be able to exercise a high level of choice concerning decisions about their lives, and that such choices be based on careful thought, analysis of relevant issues and critical evaluation of available facts and information. The Warnock Report (DES, 1978) described the following as its aims for the education of a child with special needs; 'to enable him to enter the world after formal education is over as an active participant in society and a responsible contributor to it, capable of achieving as much independence as possible' (Paragraph 1.4). Many members of society feel that acquiring literacy and numeracy skills is vital if an individual is to take his place in society in this way. It is upon these essential skills that we focus here: the basic literacy and numeracy skills a pupil *needs to be taught*.

THE TASK ANALYTIC MODEL OF CURRICULUM DEVELOPMENT

The Task Analytic Model of curriculum development is based on the principles of Task Analysis which were described in Chapter 2. Here we look in more detail at how tasks are selected for inclusion in the curriculum and how they relate to a school's overall aims of education. The steps in the curriculum model are summarised in Table 6.1.

Step 1. Select Subject Areas

Step 1 focuses on the selection of subject areas to be taught which reflect the school's long-term aims of education. They therefore cover all the subjects

Table 6.1   Task Analytic Model of Curriculum Development.

Step 1	Select subject areas
Step 2	Identify units for each subject
Step 3	Write a goal for each unit
Step 4	Write a task (as a behavioural objective) for each goal
Step 5	Analyse the task into a sequence of skills (also written as behavioural objectives)
Step 6	Slice tasks and skills (and express as behavioural objectives)
Step 7	Select order for teaching units

Steps 4-6 are where the principles of Task Analysis have been incorporated into the model.

that it is felt children must be introduced to and will include reading, arithmetic, language and writing, those areas which could collectively be viewed as comprising the core skills a pupil needs to be taught. Whilst most primary teachers would agree that teaching in these subjects is essential for all pupils, it may well be more difficult to reach a consensus over which other subjects should be viewed in this way.

Step 2. Identify Units for Each Subject

The named subject areas encompass a wide range of skills and so it is desirable to break them down into smaller areas of study. These smaller areas are referred to as units, and draw attention to the areas of learning that exist within each subject. Examples of units for the subjects reading and mathematics are shown in Table 6.2.

Table 6.2   Units for Reading and Mathematics.

Subject area	Reading	Mathematics
Units	Sight vocabulary	Language of instruction
	Phonics	Addition
	Oral language	Subtraction
	Passage reading	Multiplication
	Comprehension	Division
	Contextual analysis	Money
	Structural analysis	Time
	Study skills	Length
		Weight
		Problem solving

Units are drawn from several potential sources. They can emerge as a result of a generally agreed consensus of opinion by specialists in the subject area. There is no shortage of literature when it comes to teaching reading and arithmetic, outlining which units need to be taught. Alternatively the staff in a school may decide to write their own curriculum, and base the identification of units on a logical analysis of the subject being taught. Equally the curriculum may be based on staff discussion and represent their own collective knowledge and experience.

These pathways are not mutually exclusive and could all contribute to a school identifying units for a given subject. With complex subject areas like reading, where several theories have been postulated to account for how children learn to read, there will of course be variations in the units chosen for study, which accord to the view of reading being adopted. It is important that the units selected by the staff reflect the school's educational aims and overall philosophy of education.

Step 3. Write a Goal for Each Unit

Steps 1 and 2 of the model are concerned with identifying what is to be taught in terms of areas of study. Step 3, writing goals for each unit, represents a 'shift of focus'. This is where the areas to be studied are defined more clearly and translated into a description of skills that are to be taught. The emphasis here is on the teacher and teacher intentions.

The nature of the term 'goal' reveals the key to its identification. A goal should be seen as an end point, the final and probably most difficult skill you wish to teach for a given unit. The goal represents the point where teaching in a chosen unit ends. At present we do not have a commonly agreed basic curriculum in the United Kingdom which specifies the skills children are to be taught by various stages in their school careers. The responsibility for making such judgements rests with individual schools.

There are often many skills which a teacher might perceive as being essential for a given unit. The process by which they are identified is similar to those already described for establishing appropriate units for a subject, that is via the collected views of experts in the field, logical analysis and staff discussion. Inevitably the selection of a goal for a unit is going to be arbitrary to some extent, being governed by various influences, including, the age of the children being taught, and theoretical issues connected with the subject matter. At the primary level, expectations held by a secondary school about the skill levels required of children due to transfer, will also be an important consideration.

The starting point in articulating goals is for either individual teachers to decide for themselves, or members of staff at a school to agree collectively on the most difficult skill they wish to teach pupils within a given unit. It is not always easy to predict in advance how much you want to teach children and the possibility exists that you might underestimate what they will be able to learn. To ensure this does not happen, it is preferable to have high expectations and if necessary overestimate the skills to be taught for different units. This will have the advantage of helping to avoid the occurrence of a 'ceiling effect' whereby you run out of skills to teach. When you have a clear idea of the skill levels to be reached by pupils at different points in their school careers, predicting what they will learn is less likely to be a problem.

In Chapter 2 we gave an example of a task analysis which represented the teacher's goal of *teaching children to name colours*. This could be viewed as the most difficult skill associated with teaching children about colours. Table 6.3 shows some possible goals for the reading unit described earlier.

Table 6.3   Examples of Units and Goals From the Reading Subject Area.

Subject area	Reading
Unit ↓ Goal	Sight vocabulary ↓ Reading the 200 most commonly occurring words in written English
Unit ↓ Goal	Phonics ↓ Decoding words which contain a maximum of six different phonemes
Unit ↓ Goal	Comprehension ↓ Critically evaluating a written passage
Unit ↓ Goal	Structural analysis ↓ Decoding words formed by adding a prefix, suffix, or another word to a base word

Step 4. Write a Task (as a Behavioural Objective) for Each Goal

Goals are an expression of the skills a teacher plans to teach, where the teacher and her intentions are the focus of attention. However, it is not always immediately apparent what pupil behaviour is expected to indicate that a particular goal has been reached. Where goals have been established through staff discussion, individual teachers will have their own thoughts on what tasks they expect pupils to perform on attaining a goal. The purpose of preparing a behavioural objective is to make this process explicit and clarify precisely what a student will be able to do, in terms of her learning outcomes, to show that the goal has been reached. The behavioural objective is a statement of what a pupil has to do in order to demonstrate that a new skill has been learned. It specifies the pupil's task, the conditions under which it is presented together with criterion for successful performance. This will help to eliminate any ambiguities that may surround the nature of the task associated with a particular goal.

As well as systematising teachers' expectations of children's learning outcomes, preparing behavioural objectives has the added advantage of making it clear to children, precisely, what their tasks entail. This will help maintain their motivation to work, as they can appreciate the standard of performance they are expected to achieve.

A single behavioural objective should be written for each goal, as far as this is possible. However, there may well be some occasions when the skills contained within a single goal cannot be represented adequately with only one behavioural objective. This is most likely to occur when teaching more complex skills, particularly those associated with oral language and reading comprehension. Under these circumstances it may well be necessary to write two or more behavioural objectives for a single goal. Some examples of behavioural objectives are presented in Table 6.4.

Table 6.4   Examples of Behavioural Objectives Derived from Goals.

Goal	Reading the 200 most commonly occuring words in written English
Behavioural objective	Reads orally, the 200 most commonly occurring words in written English, when presented on flash cards on three consecutive occasions with 95% accuracy
Goal	Decoding words which contain a maximum of six different phonemes
Behavioural objective	Reads orally, phonically regular words and words with letter combinations containing between two and six phonemes (10 examples of each), when presented on flash cards, on five consecutive occasions with 95% accuracy
Goal	Critically evaluating a written passage
Behavioural objective	When presented with a passage of up to 3000 words, the pupil can state in writing (a) the author's conclusion, (b) the evidence presented, (c) the author's trustworthiness, (d) faulty arguments; on three consecutive occasions with 100% accuracy
Goal	Decoding words formed by adding a prefix, suffix or another word to base word
Behavioural objective	Reads orally and names the prefix, suffix and word base contained in 100 words formed by adding a prefix, suffix or another word to a base word, when presented on flash cards on five consecutive occasions with 95% accuracy

Writing behavioural objectives is the first step in the Task Analytic Model of Curriculum Development where the emphasis is on the pupils and their learning outcomes. Earlier steps have been concerned with the school, and how its aims are articulated as skills which teachers intend to teach. Steps 4, 5 and 6 of the process concentrate entirely on the pupils and what they should be able to do to show learning has taken place.

Step 5. Analyse the Task into a Sequence of Skills

Continuing the theme of pupil behaviour, each behavioural objective has to be looked at carefully to see how it can be broken down into a sequence of skills, each one representing a different type of activity for the pupil to be taught. The completion of this step was discussed in some detail in Chapter 2.

Step 6. Slice Tasks and Skills

There may well be some occasions when it is felt that a new task or skill is too difficult. Such circumstances would justify the task or skill being made easier but without actually changing the nature of the activity. The demands of the task are therefore reduced in some way, usually by presenting fewer examples of a difficult task for the pupil to learn. As with tasks and skills, slices are also expressed as behavioural objectives.

Before leaving the actual process of task analysis (Steps 4–6) an important point, which was alluded to earlier, needs emphasising. In many instances there will be more than one possible task analysis for a given task, especially where the task being taught is a complex one. Similarly there are often many ways in which tasks can be broken down into a series of skills. In short, there are no right and wrong task analyses, and it would take a brave person to say that one task analysis was better than another, without the justification of specific comparative research, of which there is very little. What is most important though, is that the task analysis completed by an individual teacher or members of a school staff, is one which reflects his or their own views about teaching a particular subject, and furthermore, is one which they will feel comfortable using.

Step 7. Select an Order for Teaching Units

Deciding on an order for teaching units is the final step in the Task Analytic Model. By now all the tasks and skills pupils are to be taught in a given subject area will have been clearly specified and formulated as behavioural objectives. The position has been reached where a decision can be taken about a suitable sequence for teaching each unit.

Examination of the tasks will indicate that some tasks derived from a particular unit will need to have been learned before those from another unit can be taught. They can be viewed as teaching skills which serve as pre-skills for later tasks. Imagine the situation where seven units have been identified to teach a single subject area. It might well be the case that tasks from two units teach skills which must be mastered before children can be taught tasks from a third unit. These tasks in turn must be mastered before children progress to units four, five, six and seven. Table 6.5 presents this diagrammatically.

Units are taught at four levels, each level containing some tasks which must be taught before teaching can move to the next level. However, within each level no teaching order of units can be inferred. At level I teaching could begin on tasks from unit one before unit two or vice versa. Similarly teaching at level III can start on units four, five or six.

While an order can be determined for the sequence in which teaching begins in different units, it will not be the case that all the tasks for a level I unit will be taught before progressing to level II. In reality it is likely that only some of the tasks will be covered before transferring to level II. It needs to be remembered that a unit may contain tasks which are taught over a number of years. It would not be desirable or sound teaching practice to teach them in their entirety before moving to the next level. This can be illustrated if we return to the earlier example of teaching reading. Table 6.6 shows one possible order for teaching units in reading.

Teaching reading units within this framework occurs at six levels progressing from the oral language unit at level I to study skills at level VI. Acquiring a range of oral language skills (level I) is a prerequisite for being taught sight vocabulary and phonic skills (level II). However, children who start to read when they are five years old and begin to acquire sight vocabulary and phonic skills, will certainly not yet have learned all the oral language skills that they need in later life. Nevertheless some oral language skills must be taught before progressing to level II.

Similarly, pupils will need some sight vocabulary or phonic skills before they can begin to read passages. Clearly, teaching these skills, particularly

Table 6.5 Order for Teaching Units.

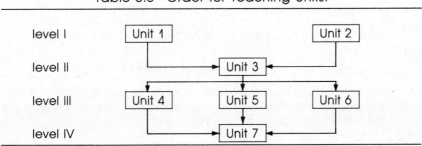

Table 6.6 Order for Teaching Reading Units.

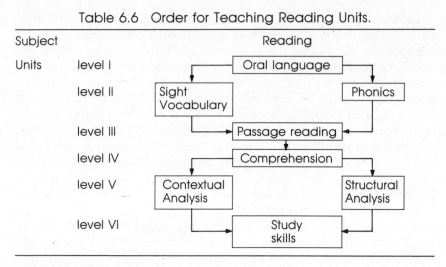

Subject   Reading

Units   level I

             level II

             level III

             level IV

             level V

             level VI

phonic skills, will extend over a number of academic years, well beyond the point at which tuition occurs at level III. This pattern is repeated for later units and levels.

The Task Analytic model described here focuses on three aspects of school life. It starts by looking at the school and the influences which are brought to bear when subject areas are included in the curriculum. The subject areas need to be narrowed down and defined more closely in terms of the key skills they encompass. Attention is then directed to the teacher and teacher intentions. The model considers how the teacher identifies skills he proposes to teach. However, knowing what you want to teach is one thing; being sure that children have been taught is another. The model therefore concludes by discussing how teacher intentions can be translated into children's learning outcomes which indicate that skills have been taught to a teacher's satisfaction.

SUMMARY

There are seven steps in the Task Analytic Model of curriculum development.

Subjects and units encompass areas of the curriculum children need to be taught and reflect a school's aims of education.

Goals describe the skills teachers intend to teach.

Steps 4–6 in the model describe how tasks are selected and analysed. They are expressed as behavioural objectives and specify children's learning outcomes.

7 DIRECT INSTRUCTION AND CURRICULUM DEVELOPMENT

OVERVIEW

This chapter describes:
— the background to preparing curricula based on the principles of Direct Instruction

— the six steps involved in designing programmes

— how a strategy is evolved to enable children to generalise what they learn

To start from scratch and prepare full and comprehensive curricula in the areas of literacy and numeracy, based on Direct Instruction principles, would be a complex process requiring a considerable amount of time. It is unrealistic to expect teachers either individually or collectively, to set time aside to undertake such an exercise. Furthermore, curricula in these areas have already been developed and we are not advocating that anyone should try to 're-invent the wheel'. Carnine and Silbert (1979) and Silbert *et al.* (1981) have described in considerable detail how curricula in reading and arithmetic have been written on the basis of Direct Instruction principles. These curricula represent many years' research and evaluation and are, to our knowledge, some of the most thoroughly prepared materials available for use in schools today. There are many attractive features of the approach which teachers may find of particular value and may well want to incorporate into their own classroom practice.

The Direct Instructionalists have been attempting to answer the question, 'What is the best way to teach each skill?' Therefore they have looked closely at the extent to which variations in curriculum design influence the effectiveness with which children can be taught. One priority in trying to tackle the question has been to try and make learning as easy as possible for pupils, and reduce the amount of information that has to be remembered. To this end every effort is made to teach children the general principles which underlie a series of problems. These are then frequently incorporated into an overall problem-solving strategy.

The curriculum designer is therefore looking for similarities between different tasks to see if they are governed by the same set of principles. Where connections can be found, a strategy is devised. When this exercise is repeated many times for different areas of the curriculum, the resulting strategies mean that children can solve a range of problems which then leads to them having less information to learn.

The emphasis given to identifying similarities and differences between tasks also enables pupils to generalise skills taught in one setting on a limited number of examples, to different settings and a much wider range of examples. While it is possible that some children would devise their own strategies and generalise skills without further teaching, Direct Instructionalists do not like to leave things to chance. They ask what happens to those pupils who do not learn strategies and to generalise for themselves? A variety of reasons could account for this but all having the same net effect: those children would be at a considerable disadvantage to their peers. The curriculum is therefore designed in such a way so as to prevent this happening and ensure that all children are taught appropriate strategies and are shown how to generalise skills.

These considerations have led to a six-step procedure for designing programmes (Table 7.1) which have been described in more detail by Carnine and Silbert (1979) and Silbert *et al.* (1981).

Table 7.1   Steps Involved in Designing Direct Instruction Programmes.

Step 1	Specifying objectives
Step 2	Devising problem-solving strategies
Step 3	Developing teaching procedures
Step 4	Selecting examples
Step 5	Providing practice
Step 6	Sequencing skills

Step 1. Specifying Objectives

In the chapter on Task Analysis we presented several reasons for specifying the skills children are to be taught in terms of behavioural objectives. A similar view is adopted within Direct Instruction about the need for a clear and unambiguous statement of what the pupil will be able to do following teaching, to indicate that learning has taken place.

Step 2. Devising Problem-solving Strategies

One of the most important features of Direct Instruction and one which makes it so widely applicable is the emphasis given to preparing problem-solving strategies.

Many strategies have been devised to teach pupils reading, mathematics, language and spelling skills. Space precludes a description of strategies drawn from each of these curricula, so we will confine our discussions to teaching arithmetic and reading. Figure 7.1 shows three arithmetic tasks that most primary teachers have responsibility for teaching at some stage during their school careers: addition, subtraction and multiplication (division is not included here as division problems are typically represented by an alternative format e.g. $3\overline{)15}$; $6\overline{)18}$ and are taught in a different way).

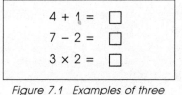

Figure 7.1 Examples of three common arithmetic tasks.

Tasks of this type are taught to pupils up and down the country almost every day of the school year, and in general, are learned by many children without too much difficulty. However, the tasks shown in Figure 7.2 frequently pose more problems, and a considerable number of students experience some difficulties in learning these operations.

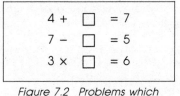

Figure 7.2 Problems which frequently cause difficulties.

Engelmann and his colleagues have looked at the tasks shown in Figures 7.1 and 7.2 and examined the skills pupils need to be taught to solve them. After various skills had been identified they continued their analysis. They wanted to know which skills were common to all the tasks represented by the three operations. They thought if this information could be identified it would be possible to teach those skills as part of an overall strategy. If this could be achieved it was anticipated that children would find the tasks much easier to learn.

Their analysis led to two skill areas being identified. Firstly completing problems in all three operations demands that children be taught *counting skills*. These skills range, at the easiest level, from rote counting (naming numerals in sequence without counting objects) to more advanced skills such as counting backwards from a number, counting on from a number and skip counting (i.e. counting in 2s, 3s, 4s, 5s, etc.). Developing counting skills to a high level is common to all the operations.

Secondly pupils need to be taught the *equality rule*. This states that in a written number problem of the type illustrated earlier, we must end with the same number to the left of the equal sign as we have on the right of the equal sign. A thorough understanding of this rule and how to apply it facilitates the processes of addition, subtraction and multiplication. The equality rule appears in the Direct Instruction arithmetic curriculum as part of a problem-solving strategy which is shown in Tables 7.2 and 7.3.

The strategy involves several key stages:
— stating the equality rule,
— knowing which side to start the problem,
— having the counting skills to complete the problem.

As children become familiar with the application of the strategy shown in Table 7.2 and learn more advanced counting skills, the problem can be

Table 7.2   Problem-Solving Strategy Incorporating Counting Skills and the Equality Rule to Teach Common Arithmetic Tasks.

(1)   The pupil is shown the problem and asked to read the equation
e.g. $3+4 = \square$, 'three plus four equals how many?'
(The answer box is always read as 'how many')

(2)   The pupil is told the equality rule which states
'we must end up with the same number on this side of the equal (circle $3+4$) and on the other side (circle the box).'

(3)   The pupil is then told something about the side he starts with
'You start with the side that tells you how many lines to draw (or objects to draw or number of concrete objects).' The pupil is informed that he cannot start on the other side because the box does not tell you how many lines to draw.

(4)   The teacher points to the first numeral, 4, and asks the pupil how many lines are required and to draw the appropriate number of lines.

(5)   The teacher points to $+3$, which tells the pupil that three more lines need to be drawn.

(6)   The pupil then counts the total number of lines.

(7)   The pupil repeats the equality rule that you must end with the same number on both sides of the equal sign and then draws seven lines under the box so that the same number is on both sides of the equal sign.

(8)   The pupil is told the lines under a box tell you what numeral goes in the box.

(9)   The pupil writes the numeral 7 in the box.
The completed sum would appear as follows

$$4 + 3 = \boxed{7}$$

completed in fewer steps. For example, pupils would not need to keep restating the equality rule, or be reminded of the correct side to start the problem. They would be able to write the numeral to balance the equation straight into the answer box. Similarly children will reach a level of skill acquisition where they can compute the problem without recourse to semi-concrete objects (lines and drawings of objects) or concrete apparatus, and will be able to count on from a numeral (e.g. in the above example they would count on from 4 and add on 3; 4, 5, 6, 7). The essential features of the strategy would remain but be carried out at greater speed.

The very same strategy also enables children to subtract and multiply with problems of the type shown in Figure 7.1. The pupil reads the equation, states the equality rule and identifies the side on which the problem is started. The difference in the strategy occurs when the sign is identified indicating which operation is to be completed.

In subtraction problems the pupil counts backwards ($7 - 2 = \square$; counts back from 7 twice; the pupil starts at 7 and counts backwards once to 6 and twice to 5); and in multiplication problems the pupil skip counts ($3 \times 2 = \square$, 'count in 3s twice'; 3 (once), 6 (twice)).

Table 7.3 illustrates how the strategy is applied to teaching missing addend problems.

Table 7.3 Strategy for Teaching Missing Addend Problems.

(1) The pupil is shown the problem and asked to read the equation e.g. $3 + \square = 8$; 'Three plus how many equals eight?'
(2) The pupil is told the equality rule which states 'We must end up with the same number on this side of the equal (circle $3 + \square$) and on the other side' (circle 8).
(3) The pupil is then told something about the side she starts with 'You start with the side that tells you how many lines to draw' (in this example to the right of the equal). The pupil is informed that he cannot start on the other side because the box does not tell you how many lines to draw.
(4) The teacher points to the 8 and asks the pupil how many lines are required and to draw the appropriate number of lines.
(5) The pupil is reminded that she must end with the same number on both sides of the equal and is asked how many are already to the left of the equal (in this example the answer being three).
(6) The pupil draws three lines under the numeral and identifies that the plus sign tells her to add on to three to reach eight.
(7) The pupil counts on from three and makes a line under the box for each number added.
(8) The pupil is asked how many to the left of the equal sign and whether the same number is on both sides of the equal.
(9) The pupil is asked how many were therefore added, counts the number of lines under the box and writes the appropriate numeral in the box.
(10) The pupil reads the whole statement.

$$3 + \boxed{5} = 8$$

Teaching the application of phonic skills is an example of a strategy used to teach reading skills. Once a pupil has been taught to read aloud the sounds for the letters *a, m, t, s, i, f, d, r, l*, the pupil can begin to blend consonant, vowel, consonant, (CVC) words on a limited set of examples, e.g. *mat, sit, ram*. Once this strategy for reading CVC words has been taught, the pupil can be presented with new examples of the skill (e.g. *sat, rat, lad, fat, fit*, etc.), where the newly acquired strategy can be applied. To teach CVC words individually as part of a sight vocabulary would not be an efficient use of teaching time, and would demand that a student memorises far more information than is desirable or necessary.

Step 3. Developing Teaching Procedures

It is important when teaching children who are experiencing learning difficulties to ensure that there is a high level of consistency in the teaching approach from day to day. This requires making sure the instructions to children are well thought out, directly related to the task being taught and open to only one interpretation. Verbal instructions to pupils are all too frequently thought up on the spur of the moment and are not given the planning time they deserve (Junkula, 1972).

The Direct Instruction model rejects the belief that as many different approaches as possible should be tried for teaching a single task in the hope that the pupil will learn from one of them. This orientation is unlikely to result in maximally effective instruction. The danger is the pupil will not learn through any of the approaches, since all that tends to happen is the pupil becomes increasingly confused and may well learn several different ways of *how not* to complete the task. Therefore Direct Instruction advocates that only one approach should be used at a time and that its effects should be carefully monitored. It is further advocated that it is the teacher's responsibility to select the most appropriate teaching procedure for a particular task, and is not a decision which should by default be 'left to children to make'.

There are two stages to any teaching procedure, an *introduction stage* and a *discrimination stage*. During the introduction stage there is a high level of pupil–teacher interaction as the teacher demonstrates the steps in a problem-solving strategy and provides the pupil with structured practice sessions. During the discrimination stage, the pupil works independently on examples which require the student to discriminate between using the new strategy, and different, previously taught strategies.

Step 4. Selecting Examples

Examples are prepared for the introduction and discrimination stages of learning. During the introduction stage only examples requiring the application of the newly taught strategy are presented. In the example of teaching pupils to decode consonant, vowel, consonant (CVC) words, children are only asked to read words for which they had already been taught the appropriate letter–sound correspondences. Where a pupil had learned the letters *a*, *m*, *t*, *s*, *r*, and *i*, words used to teach decoding skills would include *sat*, *sit*, *ram*, etc. They would not include the words, *met*, *rut*, etc., as the sounds *e* and *u* had not yet been taught.

Selecting items for the discrimination stage should be seen as an opportunity for reviewing previously taught skills. Pupils will be expected to use newly acquired skills and discriminate them from examples of other skills they have been taught. When children are learning to blend CVCe words (e.g. *mate*, *bite*, etc) the discrimination stage requires that these words are discriminated from a similar skill learned earlier, perhaps CVC words or CVCC words (e.g. *camp*, *lost*, etc).

Step 5. Providing Practice

Learning any new skill requires a considerable amount of practice. In the initial phase of teaching the pupils should be provided with concentrated practice. In time, and as new skills are introduced, there will be less intensive practice, as a section of each lesson is devoted to revising what they have learned to check if it has been retained. Without practice and regular reviews it is unlikely that important skills will be retained over time.

Step 6. Sequencing Skills

If skills are to be well taught, considerable thought needs to be given to the order in which new information is presented to pupils. Five guidelines are used in Direct Instruction, which if followed, should help to increase the rate at which pupils learn.

Pre-skills of a strategy are taught before the strategy itself. Before a strategy can be taught, it is essential that the individual components of the strategy have been learned by the pupil. Thus, when teaching the strategy for addition to 10, pre-skills which need to be taught include counting to 10, one-to-one correspondence, naming numerals, writing numerals and equation reading, etc.

Instances that are consistent with a strategy are introduced before exceptions. Positive instances of a strategy are always presented before any exceptions. This will help eliminate confusion on the pupil's part by ensuring that regular examples of the strategy are well taught prior to the introduction of exceptions. This applies particularly when teaching letter combinations such as the vowel digraph, '*oo*'. The '*oo*' combination occurs more frequently in words like '*moon*' than in words like '*book*', therefore the former sound for the '*oo*' combination is taught before the latter sound.

Useful skills are introduced before less useful ones. This principle provides the basis for introducing new sight vocabulary to pupils. High frequency words which are likely to occur in many different reading schemes (e.g. *was, are, as, she*) are taught before less frequently occurring sight vocabulary (e.g. *while, bus, family*).

Easier skills are taught before more difficult ones. Teaching easier skills before more difficult ones has particular implications when children are taught to blend CVC words. Words which have a continuous sound (e.g. *s*, *m*, *r*, *f*, *n*, etc.) in the initial consonant position (e.g. *sat, men, ran*) are easier to blend than those having a stop sound (*b, c, d, t, p* etc.) in the initial consonant position (e.g. *bit, cat, dog*). They should therefore be taught first.

Strategies and information that are likely to be confused are not introduced at the same time. It is always advisable to separate the teaching of skills which are likely to be confused. For example, when teaching letter sounds, some groups of letters might be difficult to teach because of their visual (*b*, *p*, *d*) or auditory (*e*, *i*) similarity. It is advocated therefore that these groups of letters are not taught together and should only be presented with each other after they have been learned separately. This will reduce the likelihood of them being mixed up.

SUMMARY

Direct Instruction programmes are designed to teach children with learning difficulties how to generalise what they are taught.

Six steps are involved in designing programmes.

Children learn to generalise through being taught problem-solving strategies.

Teaching procedures are systematically evaluated.

Skills are sequenced according to five main principles.

RECOMMENDED FURTHER READING

Becker, W. C., Engelmann, S. and Thomas, D. R. (1975). *Teaching 2: Cognitive Learning and Instruction*. S.R.A., Chicago.

Bereiter, C. and Engelmann, S. (1966). *Teaching Disadvantaged Children in the Preschool*. Prentice Hall, New Jersey.

Engelmann, S., Haddox, P. and Bruner, E. (1983). *Teach Your Child to Read in 100 Easy Lessons*. Simon and Schuster, New York.

8 EVALUATING AND ADAPTING PUBLISHED MATERIALS

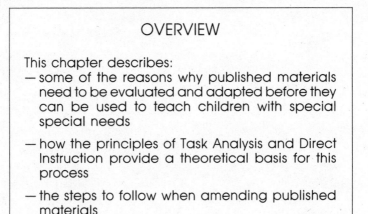

OVERVIEW

This chapter describes:
— some of the reasons why published materials
  need to be evaluated and adapted before they
  can be used to teach children with special
  special needs

— how the principles of Task Analysis and Direct
  Instruction provide a theoretical basis for this
  process

— the steps to follow when amending published
  materials

There are times when published materials comprise the backbone of
the curriculum. They are prepared by experienced primary teachers of
reading and mathematics who offer a series of tasks to be taught, and
accompanying suggestions on appropriate teaching methods. Such schemes
can provide a valuable lifeline in those first few, nerve-wracking, months
of a new teaching career, and many children will benefit and make good
progress in response to teaching with these materials. However, in our
experience some children do not make the kind of progress of which
they are capable, despite the published programmes being taught skilfully
and enthusiastically. Some of the reasons for this relate specifically to
the materials being used.

Any scheme of work taken directly from the shelf will need to be looked
at carefully before being used to teach children experiencing difficulties. In
this chapter we illustrate how the principles of Task Analysis and Direct
Instruction are applied when evaluating and adapting a scheme of work.
However, we begin by considering some of the factors which can limit the
effectiveness of published materials.

ISSUES TO CONSIDER WHEN EVALUATING
AND ADAPTING PUBLISHED MATERIALS

Sequencing of Skills

The order in which literacy and numeracy skills are sequenced is a crucial factor in determining how successfully they are learned. When looking at a published curriculum you are faced with trying to answer the question: 'By what criteria can a skill sequence be judged suitable for teaching children with learning difficulties?' Several areas need to be considered.

It is likely that the presented skill sequence will be based on particular theoretical perspectives. When teaching reading, these might include look–say, phonic or language experience approaches. You would need to ask how well the sequence represented a specific theoretical framework. Does the sequence seem logical according to the model used and your own experience? How finely are the tasks broken down? Is more than one skill taught at a time? The answers to these questions will help in formulating an opinion on the likely value of the curriculum being assessed.

Task Specification

How clearly specified are the tasks that the children have to learn? We have already indicated that an important element in curriculum preparation for children with learning difficulties is a clear and unambiguous statement of what they are expected to do, to show that learning has taken place. Where it is not clear what a task entails, behavioural objectives should be prepared outlining the three key elements; pupil task, conditions and criteria for mastery.

Problem-solving Strategies

Children will learn more quickly and efficiently if they can be taught strategies which enable them to complete a range of tasks. This is certainly preferable to teaching children skills which rely heavily on memorising large numbers of facts. Guidelines for teaching problem-solving strategies need to be prepared if none are given in the teacher's manual accompanying the scheme.

Presenting New Skills

Both teacher and pupil will be helped if materials include a worked example which shows how to complete a task when it is taught for the first time. The example would illustrate the steps to be followed in some detail, which can subsequently act as a reminder to the pupil.

Number of Examples

Schemes of work should provide sufficient examples of the skill being taught, to allow children to have intensive periods of practice so they can increase their fluency. Some pupils will master the skill following a brief teaching session and with little practice. Others will require teaching over several days with greater opportunities for practice to occur.

For example, in Level 1 Book 5 of Mathematics for Schools (Howell *et al.*, 1981) children are introduced to matching tasks. During the course of the book pupils are required to match two, three, four and five objects respectively. Table 8.1 shows the number of practice items presented for each set of objects which need to be matched.

Table 8.1 Number of Practice Items Presented to Teach Matching Skills in Level 1 Book 5 of Mathematics for Schools.

Number of objects to be matched	Number of practice items
2	5
3	4
4	2
5	2

A teacher intending to teach the above tasks using the Mathematics for Schools scheme needs to decide whether the number of practice items presented is sufficient. In this particular instance we would anticipate that most teachers would think not, and that this may well be true of many areas within a scheme of work. Where this is the case, supplementary materials should be prepared.

Criteria for Mastery

To be sure that children have mastered a skill, the teacher needs clear guidelines on the level of performance required to indicate that mastery has been achieved. Unfortunately it cannot be automatically assumed that completing all the examples will necessarily promote mastery. It is particularly unlikely that desired fluency levels will have been reached. In the absence of published criteria levels it is necessary for teachers to specify their own.

Instructions to Teachers

Ideally for schemes of work to be maximally effective, the teacher needs guidelines on how to use the materials which point out:
— what the aim of teaching the task is,
— the task the pupil has to perform,

— the materials required to teach the task,

— criterion for successful performance.

Very few manuals for published materials include details on all of these areas. Therefore it can be extremely valuable for staff to discuss these issues before they begin teaching, so they can feel confident about *what*, *why*, and *how* they are going to teach.

Instructions for the Pupil

It is helpful if the teacher's manual outlines the instructions to be given to pupils when teaching each task. These should take account of previously used vocabulary and only include words which have already been taught to the pupil. Preparing instructions in advance has the distinct advantage of freeing the teacher to concentrate on presenting the task enthusiastically and skilfully, rather than thinking up instructions as he goes along.

Many schemes of work cannot be used without some amendments to tailor them to the particular circumstances of teachers and children in an individual school. Much preparatory work will be involved in order to make the necessary adaptations. A good deal of supplementary materials need to be prepared as a back-up to children who do not master tasks within the number of examples presented in the student workbooks. Furthermore, instructions will need to be clarified and criteria established.

STEPS IN EVALUATING AND ADAPTING PUBLISHED MATERIALS

The rest of this chapter introduces and describes a seven-step procedure (Table 8.2) for preparing a curriculum based on existing published materials. The procedure draws on the principles of Task Analysis and Direct Instruction.

Table 8.2 Steps in Evaluating and Adapting a Curriculum From Published Materials.

Step 1	List the skills and tasks to be taught in the order presented in the scheme
Step 2	Evaluate the curriculum sequence
Step 3	Revise the sequence of skills and tasks
Step 4	Write behavioural objectives for each task
Step 5	Devise problem-solving strategies
Step 6	Devise teaching procedures
Step 7	Prepare examples for practice

Step 1. List the Skills to be Taught
in the Order Presented in the Scheme

The teacher's manual accompanying a scheme usually lists the skills to be taught, and gives guidelines on appropriate teaching methods. After studying the manual, it should be possible to identify a sequence for teaching the listed skills. Figure 8.1 shows a record form that could be used to display the necessary information. This particular form provides space for displaying the essential details of the skills being taught, and where they can be located in the scheme. The final column is included so that the number of practice items presented throughout the scheme can be noted at a glance, to give a quick indication of where supplementary materials might need to be prepared.

Skills to be taught	Sequence of tasks	Example of task	Book and page number	Number of practice items

Figure 8.1   Record form for listing skills and tasks taught in published materials.

Alternative forms could be devised which would include additional information. For example, a more comprehensive display would note the author's reasons for including each skill taught, and may also refer to various aspects of the suggested teaching methods. The main consideration in preparing a record form is that it contains all the information you feel is important in helping you evaluate the scheme of work under review.

Some teachers' manuals have scope and sequence charts which give a brief introduction to the skills taught, and the order in which they are presented. While these can serve a useful purpose when a quick inspection of skill sequences employed is required, they do not generally contain sufficient information to be helpful in preparing the detailed type of skill sequence being suggested here.

Tables 8.3 and 8.4 respectively, present partially completed examples of a couple of record forms used when evaluating and adapting published arithmetic and reading schemes.

Table 8.3 Adapting a Published Arithmetic Scheme.

Skills to be taught	Sequence of tasks	Example	Book and page numbers	Number of practice items
Addition to 10	n+ n	4+ 3	Bk 2; pp.7 – 9	30
	n+ ☐ =6	3+ ☐ =6	Bk 3; pp 24 – 5	9
	n+n= ☐	5+5= ☐	Bk 3; pp 15 – 16	15
Addition to 20	n+n= ☐	7+5= ☐	Bk 4; pp 11, 14	17
Adding three numerals	n+ n+ n	6+ 5+ 3	Bk 6; p 3	7
Addition of TU (no renaming)	no+no= ☐	20+30= ☐	Bk 6; p 9	5
	nn+n= ☐	42+6= ☐	Bk 6; pp 12, 13	21
	nn+ nn	28+ 51	Bk 6; p 24	30
Addition of TU (renaming)	nc+ nn	37+ 49	Bk 7; p 5	23
	nc+ nn+ nn	26+ 15+ 34	Bk 7; pp 12, 13, 17	27
Addition HTU (no renaming)	nnn+ nnn	128+ 131	Bk 8; p 19	12
Addition HTU (renaming)	nnc+ nnn	126+ 137	Bk 9; pp 2, 3	15
	ncn+ nnn	184+ 693	Bk 9; p 9	20
	ncc+ nnn	177+ 528	Bk 9; p 10	6

Note: (a) n represents a numeral between 0-9.

(b) nn+ represents the addition of two numbers where the total in the units
 n
column does not exceed 9 (i.e no renaming) e.g. 21+
 3

(c) nc+ represents the addition of two numbers where the total in the units
 n
column does exceed 9 (i.e. renaming required) e.g. 47+
 5

(d) no+ represents the addition of two numbers where the first number has a
 n
zero in the units column e.g. 40+
 6

Table 8.4 Adapting a Published Reading Scheme.

Skills to be taught	Sequence of tasks	Example	Book and page numbers	Number of examples
Phonics: Letter sounds	a–z	not applicable	not applicable	not applicable
Phonics: regular phonic words	VC	it	Bk 2 pp 3, 4, 5, 7, 9, 10, 11	17
	CVC	men	Bk 3 pp 4 – 18	24
Phonics: letter combinations	th	bath	Bk 5 pp 1 – 12	14
	ch	chop	Bk 5 pp 17 – 20	5
	wh	whip	Bk 5 pp 21 – 24	8
	ea	beat	Bk 5 pp 26 – 29	7
	ee	peel	Bk 6 pp 2 – 7	11
	oo	fool	Bk 6 pp 8 – 15	11
	ai	paid	Bk 6 pp 17 – 20	7
	ou	loud	Bk 6 pp 22 – 27	4
Phonics: regular phonic words	CVCC	bend	Bk 7 pp 1 – 12	22
	CCVC	slip	Bk 7 pp 7 – 19	11
	CCVCC	brand	Bk 8 pp 2 – 8	10

Note: (a) C represents a consonant
      (b) V represents a vowel

Step 2. Evaluate the Curriculum Sequence

The sequencing guidelines derived from Task Analysis and Direct Instruction provide a basis for evaluating a curriculum sequence. In Task Analysis, the aim is to sequence easier tasks before more difficult ones, since it is anticipated that learning the earlier tasks in a sequence, will facilitate the pupil's learning of later and relatively more complex tasks.

The principles of Direct Instruction reiterate this point and add that:
— more useful tasks are taught before less useful tasks,
— tasks which may be confused are not taught together.
We can look at the extracts from the two curricular sequences in the light of these guidelines and search for instances where they have or have not been adhered to. Changes, if necessary, can occur in two places. Firstly the order in which skills are to be taught might be altered. Secondly, the sequence of tasks for a given skill could be amended.

In most instances the curricular sequences correspond to the recommended principles. However, changes could be made in the following areas in the arithmetic scheme:

— *change the order in which skills are taught*. Group together all the problems which do not require renaming (e.g. addition of TU and addition of HTU). Similarly regroup the problems which do require renaming so they are all taught together. Rearranging the skills in this way will make it easier to devise an effective problem-solving strategy.

— *change the sequence of tasks for a given skill*. The sequence for teaching addition to ten could be altered so that the series starts with adding two numerals, presented horizontally, before attempting the missing addend problems. The principles of Direct Instruction remind us to try and teach just one skill at a time so the vertically presented task would be omitted at this stage. We can then concentrate on teaching the skills of addition, and not risk the pupil becoming confused by a different type of presentation.

— *insert a task*. The vertical addition of two numerals could now be taught as a pre-skill for adding three numerals.

The following changes could be made in the reading scheme:

— *teach more useful tasks before less useful tasks*. An alternative to teaching letter sounds in alphabetic sequence is to sequence them according to their usefulness. Sounds such as *m*, *t*, *s*, and *i* occur in many regular phonic words and should ideally be introduced to children earlier rather than later, so they can progress quickly, to being taught blending skills.

— *re-sequence tasks which may be confused*. The final change would be to reconsider the order in which some of the letter combinations are taught. Those that are visually (*ch*, *th*, *wh*) or auditorally similar, (*ea*, *ee*) should be introduced separately as they might well be confusing for many pupils.

As well as altering the sequence of skills and tasks taught, the option of adding or omitting skill areas and tasks to a published curriculum also exists. The principles of Task Analysis might dictate that important skill areas have been excluded. Equally, it may be felt that tasks have been included which do not facilitate the learning of later tasks in the sequence and should therefore be left out.

Step 3. Revise the Sequence of Skills and Tasks

Once the scheme has been examined it will become apparent whether changes need to be made in the sequence of skills and tasks. There has been lamentably little research into skill sequences on which to base definitive judgements about preferred ordering. Ultimately the most valid conclusions about a given sequence can be drawn after it has been used to teach pupils. Moreover, if children who had previously failed to master skills, learn them quickly and efficiently by following a particular sequence, encouraging conclusions could be drawn about the order in which the skills had been taught.

Following the analysis of arithmetic and reading curricula, examples of revised sequences are shown in Tables 8.5 and 8.6.

Table 8.5   Revised Arithmetic Teaching Order.

Skill to be taught	Sequence of tasks	Example
Addition to 10	n+n= ☐ n+ ☐ =n	3+2= ☐ 4+ ☐ =9
Addition to 20	n+n= ☐	8+9= ☐
Vertical addition: two numerals	n n̲+	7 7̲+
three numerals	n+ n+ n̲	8+ 7+ 6̲
Addition of TU (no renaming)	no+no= ☐ nn+n= ☐ nn+ nn̲	50+20= ☐ 23+3= ☐ 46+ 21̲
Addition HTU (no renaming)	nnn+ nnn̲	143+ 342̲
Addition TU (renaming)	nc+ nn̲	27+ 49̲
	nc+ nn+ nn̲	43+ 39+ 12̲
Addition HTU (renaming)	nnc+ nnn̲	324+ 368̲
	ncn+ nnn̲	582+ 271̲
	ncc+ nnn̲	695+ 199̲

Step 4. Write Behavioural Objectives for Each Task

We discussed the need for clear unambiguous statements of pupil performance in Chapter 2. Behavioural objectives should therefore be written to accompany each task. In many cases when teaching literacy and numeracy skills, the objective can take the form of a probe, the timed test derived from the principles of Precision Teaching. More will be said of probe construction and setting criteria in Chapter 14 on Precision Teaching.

Table 8.6 Revised Reading Teaching Order.

Skill to be taught	Sequence of tasks	Example
Phonics: letter sounds	a, m, t, s, i f, d, r, o, g l, h, u, c, b, n, k, v, e, p, w, j, y, x, q, z.	not applicable
Phonics: regular phonic words	VC CVC CVCC CCVC CCVCC	in sat mast drop clamp
Phonics: letter combinations	th ea oo ch ai ee ou wh	think seat boot chip pain feet foul whip

Step 5 and Step 6. Devise Problem-solving Strategies and Teaching Procedures

The benefits of preparing problem-solving strategies and teaching procedures were discussed in the introduction to Direct Instruction. The strategies and teaching procedures used can be adapted from other schemes, or could be prepared specifically for the materials in use when no alternative exists.

Step 7. Prepare Examples for Practice

The final step involves augmenting the existing materials with a sufficient number of examples of the new skill for children to practise on. The final column of Tables 8.3 and 8.4 indicates the extent to which practice items have been incorporated into the schemes we showed as examples. By carefully examining this column and drawing upon previous experience in teaching tasks, it will become clear where additional examples need to be developed.

Published materials do, from time to time, form the basis of the curriculum in given subject areas. Whilst they have much to recommend them, there are a number of factors which can limit their effectiveness when teaching children with special needs. As a result they need to be carefully reviewed and amended before being used in the classroom. In this chapter we have discussed how the principles of Task Analysis and Direct Instruction provide guidelines which enable existing materials to be evaluated and adapted.

SUMMARY

Published materials need to be evaluated and adapted before they can be used with children with special needs.

The principles of Task Analysis and Direct Instruction provide the framework for this review.

They emphasise the need to;

— examine the sequence in which skills are taught so that there is a natural progression from the easier to more difficult tasks.

— check that tasks are grouped together in such a way so that they can be taught by problem-solving strategies.

— write behavioural objectives (which can be in the form of probes) which clarify what the child's tasks are and specify criteria for mastery.

— prepare supplementary materials to ensure enough practice items are available for the children to practice on.

RECOMMENDED FURTHER READING

Siegel, E. and Siegel, M. S. (1975). Ten Guidelines For Writing Instructional Sequences. *Journal of Learning Disabilities*, **8**, 4, 15–21.

PART III
Deciding What to Teach and How to Teach

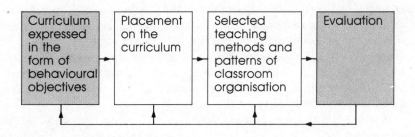

9 PLACEMENT ON THE CURRICULUM

OVERVIEW

This chapter describes:
— why commercially available criterion-referenced tests are, in general, not suitable for placing children on the curriculum
— the principles behind placement probing, a procedure for placing children on the curriculum
— the steps involved in placement probing

Before any teaching can take place, the child must be correctly placed on the curriculum. At the beginning of a new school year some information will probably be available, in the form of records passed on by a previous teacher. However, over a long summer holiday children will have plenty of time to forget what had been taught during the summer months. So although these records can serve as an invaluable guide, it must be remembered that details may have changed since their completion. Also during the year when a child is having specific difficulties on a task, the teacher may well want to double check that the work set is at an appropriate level of difficulty. In either case, the busy class teacher needs a quick, easy and efficient way of ensuring that children are placed correctly on the curriculum.

Typically when teachers and psychologists have wanted to know which skills children have or have not learned in a particular subject area, they have used criterion-referenced tests. These tests compare a pupil's performance on a series of tasks, representing a range of skills, to pre-specified criterion levels. If the criterion is reached the skill is said to have been learned; where the criterion has not been met, further teaching in that skill area would be assumed necessary. Whilst criterion-referenced tests have much to recommend them, those available commercially are not suitable for our purposes here. The main reason for this is they are not sufficiently *curriculum sensitive*. That is, the skills on which they test children's competence may well not be the skills that you or your colleagues have been teaching and which are included in the school's curriculum. The reverse of this situation also occurs where the skills taught are not to be found in the commercial test.

Within the process of Curriculum Based Assessment the criterion-referenced tests have to mirror the curriculum used in the school. This means they must be 'home-produced' by school staff and represent the skills taught in the curriculum. We are going to introduce a particularly effective way of doing this which draws on the principles of Precision Teaching and which is known as *placement probing*.

Placement probes are a series of probes which sample a pupil's skill levels on a number of key tasks drawn from the curriculum. They provide the teacher with information on children's fluency as well as accuracy and so tell us which tasks have been mastered and which have not. Furthermore, they are quick and easy to administer as each probe usually lasts for no longer than one minute. They are therefore an extremely effective way of pinpointing exactly where the child is on the curriculum, and identifying what should be taught next. The process of placement probing we describe has five steps which are summarised in Table 9.1.

Table 9.1   Steps Involved in Placement Probing.

Step 1	Select the skills to probe
Step 2	Write probes for each group of skills
Step 3	Plan how to administer the placement probes
Step 4	Plan how to score and record performance
Step 5	Determine rules for making placement decisions

Step 1. Select the Skills to Probe

The busy class teacher will not have time to give probes to assess an individual pupil's competence on each skill in a given curriculum area, especially when some areas may require between 100 and 200 different skills to be taught. Instead the child's progress can be checked on a smaller number of skills, which are representative of the entire curriculum. We can illustrate how this might happen by looking at Table 9.2 which lists the phonic skills which Carnine and Silbert (1979) suggest should comprise a phonics curriculum. Also shown is how the skills can be grouped for placement probing.

Step 2. Write Probes for Each Group of Skills

Seven probes could be written which, when taken together contain examples of all 43 skills taught in the curriculum, ranging from the easier, earlier skills (letter sounds and VC words) to the less frequently occurring and more difficult

Table 9.2 A Phonics Curriculum and Suggested Placement Probes.

Skill	Example	Placement Probe
Letter sounds	a–z	Probe 1
VC	an, on, .	
CVC	sit, man, run	
CVCC	bend, sink	
CCVC	plod, grim	
CCVCC	stamp, blend	Probe 2
CCCVC	strum	
CCCVCC	string	
CVCe	pane, pole	
CCVCe	bride, grape	
ll	fall, call	
ck	pack, lick	
th	them, this	
er	fern, perm	
ing	sing, ring	Probe 3
sh	shop, wish	
wh	whip, when	
qu	quilt	
ol	bold, volt	
ar	farm, cart	
ea	beat, lead	
oo	fool, boot	
ee	free, see	Probe 4
ai	claim	
ch	chip, rich	
or	corn, lord	
ay	day, ray	
igh	fight, high	
ow	crow	
ur	burn, surf	
oa	boat, cloak	
au	fault,	Probe 5
ou	loud, clout	
aw	claw, jaw	
ir	bird, shirt	
kn	knit	
oi	coin, soil	
ph	graph	
ey	hockey	Probe 6
wr	wrap	
ue	blue	
oy	boy, joy	
ew	flew	
All skills from VC to ew (42)	Combination of probes 2–6	Probe 7

skills (the letter combinations *oy*, *ew*). (Details of how phonic probes are designed can be found in Chapter 11). Probe 1 consists of all 26 letters, Probe 2 contains a randomised mixture of VC, CVC, CVCC, CCVC, CCVCC, CCCVC, CCCVCC, CVCe and CCVCe words where each skill appears an equal number of times. Probe 3 contains a randomised mixture of words containing, *ll*, *ck*, *th*, *er*, *ing*, *sh*, *wh*, *qu* and *ol*, with Probes 4, 5, 6 and 7 constructed in a similar way. If the above probes are administered to a child using one minute timings, an indication of the pupil's performance across this range of curriculum tasks could be established within seven minutes probing (or testing) time, a very quick and efficient way of determining what has been taught. In reality slightly longer would probably be required to allow each pupil to receive appropriate feedback and praise for their efforts.

Fewer or more placement probes could be written depending on:
— the number of pupils to be given probes and thus the time available,
— the number of skills likely to be taught during the course of an academic year.

If you anticipated that only the skills from letter sounds through to teaching '*ol*' were going to be covered (19 skills instead of 43), a different set of placement probes could be constructed to sample pupil performance on these 19 skills only. The procedure is eminently flexible, serving to sample pupil performance on a *range of skills of the teacher's choosing*.

Step 3. Plan How to Administer the Placement Probes

Deciding how best to administer placement probes is no different from planning any other form of individualised work with a child, whether this be listening to them read, explaining a new teaching point, or talking to a pupil who wishes to discuss something that has captured his imagination. In each case the classroom has to be well organised and arrangements made to ensure other children have work to do.

Several areas need to be considered during the planning stage to minimise the likelihood of interruptions (see Table 9.3). Nevertheless, teaching being

Table 9.3 Points to Consider when Planning to Administer Placement Probes.

The number of children giving cause for concern.
The duration of placement probing.
The time of day when placement probing is to start.
The work to be undertaken by children not given the probes.
The conditions under which the placement probes will be given.

the job it is, even the best laid plans could not cover every possible course of events. However, we hope that most of them can be anticipated.

We can look at how the issues raised when planning to administer placement probes, might be treated practically, by considering the example of Mr Roberts, a teacher who gave the phonic placement probes shown in Table 9.2, to two children in his class at the beginning of the new school year. These are the decisions he took.

Number of children. There were two children in the class, Susan and Michael, whose progress had been a cause of concern to their previous teacher. The records handed on indicated that they had experienced particular difficulties in learning phonic skills. Mr Roberts therefore decided to give the children the seven placement probes.

Duration. Mr Roberts calculated that the minimum time required to administer the placement probes would be 14 minutes, seven minutes for Susan and seven minutes for Michael. He also recognised that as probing was a new procedure to the children, extra time would have to be allowed to make them feel at ease and to offer praise and encouragement upon completion of each probe. Mr Roberts allocated time to check the work of the rest of the class and answer queries between probing Susan and Michael. Altogether Mr Roberts decided he would need approximately half an hour to give all the probes.

Time of day. Mr Roberts thought the children would work best if they were given the probes during the morning session before playtime. He scheduled probing to start at 9.20 a.m. and planned to finish at about 9.50 a.m.

Work for the class. Altogether there were 30 children in the class who were arranged in six, equal-sized, mixed-ability groups. During the placement probing each group was given a series of activities to work on, which did not require any teacher assistance so that those children being probed could receive maximum attention.

Administering the placement probes. Mr Roberts planned to sit at his desk in a position where he could see all the children in the class. Susan and Michael would come out in turn, when requested, to be given their probes. The rest of the class would be asked to complete the activities which they had been given and which were written on the blackboard. The tasks were carefully selected so that children could work quietly on their own and would have little difficulty in finishing them. Although no problems were anticipated, the children were reminded not to interrupt Mr Roberts whilst Susan and Michael were in the middle of a probe. They were asked to wait until Mr Roberts was free to help them and then put up their hands to seek his assistance.

Step 4. Plan How to Score and Record Performance

When children are placed on the curriculum using a series of placement probes, their results will always be scored in terms of the frequency of correct and incorrect responses made per minute. In most basic skill areas there is little difficulty in determining whether a given response was correct or incorrect, and this is helped by adopting certain probing conventions.

The first is that if a response has not been attempted within five seconds (when the probe length used is one minute), the child is moved on to the next item and an error is recorded. This ensures that the pupil has the opportunity of making a minimum of 12 responses per minute. Similarly, a pupil is moved on when an item has been attempted but not completed within five seconds. This item is then counted as an error. The final convention allows a student to self-correct a response if the correction occurs within five seconds of being made. Using these conventions provides a clear understanding of what constitutes correct and incorrect responses and enables students' probe sheets to be marked easily.

Pupils' results can then be written on a record sheet (Table 9.4). It contains space for all the important information to be entered. The skills tested are noted in the appropriate boxes, pupils' correct responses being written under the column headed by a tick, and the errors written under the column headed by a cross.

Table 9.4   Class Record Sheet for Administering Placement Probes.

School_____ Subject _____		Class_____ Date _____		Teacher _____					
Name of pupil	Chron- ological age	Skills							
		√ x	√ x	√ x	√ x	√ x	√ x	√ x	√ x

Step 5. Determine Rules for Making Placement Decisions

The identification of those skills which have been mastered depends on the criteria adopted for successful performance. This subject will be discussed in some detail in Chapter 14. In our example of phonic placement probing, we have adopted a criterion for mastery of 50 correct responses per minute with no more than two errors per minute. Table 9.5 shows the results of the seven placement probes.

According to our criterion Susan has mastered the skills included in Probes 1 and 2 but not in Probe 3. Here she completed the probe with a high level of accuracy making only two errors. However, she was still some way short of the desired criterion of 50 correct responses. On Probes 4–7, Susan recorded high error rates with the number of correct responses again well below the chosen criterion level. The teacher now has to draw this information together. There would be no need to teach skills drawn from Probes 1 and 2 since they had already been learned, whereas skills drawn from Probes 4–7 appeared too difficult. Teaching would thus commence on the skills included in Probe 3.

Table 9.5   A Completed Record Sheet.

School A Subject Phonics		Class Y Date 4th September					Teacher Mr. Roberts	
Name of pupil	Chron-ological age	Skills						
		Probe 1	Probe 2	Probe 3	Probe 4	Probe 5	Probe 6	Probe 7
		√ x	√ x	√ x	√ x	√ x	√ x	√ x
Susan	7 years 6 months	**83 0**	**56 2**	35 2	15 12	14 17	10 21	15 15
Michael	7 years 6 months	**94 1**	**68 2**	**57 1**	**56 0**	45 2	21 7	19 10

The teacher might well start by giving Susan individual probes for the nine skills represented in Probe 3 (ll, ck, th, er, ing, sh, wh, qu, ol) to see if any of the letter combinations had already been mastered. This would direct attention to skills she had not learned. Alternatively the teacher might progress through each letter combination in sequence starting with ll and finishing with ol, spending time teaching the skills not yet taught and providing some revision on any skill that Susan had already learned.

In the case of Michael the criterion level was reached on Probes 1–4. The teacher would thus be happy that the skills they incorporate had been performed with proficiency. However, further teaching would be required on Probes 5, 6 and 7. The teacher would start on the eight letter combinations covered by Probe 5. The option exists, as it did with Susan, of giving individual probes for the eight phonic skills and identifying specific skills which require further instruction. Alternatively teaching may start immediately with the first skill, *igh* and progress systematically to the final skill, *ir*, providing additional teaching or opportunities for revision, as appropriate.

One of the aims of this book is to stress the benefits of advanced planning, principally in preventing difficulties occurring in the future. By following a systematic procedure for placing children accurately on the curriculum, later problems which invariably arise when children are given work which is too easy or difficult, will probably be prevented. There are various methods of curriculum placement, none of which though, is as quick, reliable or effective as placement probing, for determining which skills children have and have not been taught. The approach is flexible in its application and, perhaps most importantly, it mirrors exactly the curriculum being used by a school.

SUMMARY

Children need to be accurately placed on the curriculum before teaching can start.

Commercially available criterion-referenced tests are usually not sufficiently curriculum sensitive to allow this to be done with confidence.

Placement probes, based on the principles of Precision Teaching, mirror the curriculum a school uses and ensure children are accurately placed on the curriculum.

Five steps are involved in placement probing which cover; selecting skills for probing, writing and administering probes, recording performance and finally making placement decisions.

RECOMMENDED FURTHER READING

Alper, T., Nowlin, L., Lemoine, K., Perine, M. and Bettencourt, B. (1973). The Rated Assessment of Academic Skills. *Academic Therapy*, **9**, 1, 151–164.

Johnson, M. S. and Kress, R. A. (1971). Task Analysis for Criterion-Referenced Tests. *The Reading Teacher*, **24**, 2, 355–359.

10 DECIDING HOW TO TEACH

```
┌─────────────────────────────────────────────────┐
│                    OVERVIEW                       │
│                                                   │
│  This chapter describes:                          │
│  — the Instructional Hierarchy                    │
│                                                   │
│  — the recommeded teaching procedures for         │
│    each stage in the Hierarchy                    │
│                                                   │
│  — Direct Instruction teaching procedures         │
└─────────────────────────────────────────────────┘
```

An alternative, perhaps slightly less familiar, way of looking at the subject of children with special needs, is that it is not so much about *teaching children with learning difficulties, but helping teachers with teaching difficulties*. Children who are failing inevitably present a challenge to the busy class teacher and her expertise. It is easy to see the reasons for this. A common expectation when planning to teach children with difficulties, is that it is inevitably going to be time consuming, that children are going to need individualised teaching with one-to-one attention. How can sufficient time be found in a typically busy school day to provide the help required?

From our experience such thoughts are invariably uppermost in the minds of many teachers. However, this view is in danger of becoming part of educational mythology. Although it contains an element of truth, since planning and preparation time is certainly required, only a small part of an effective programme is ever likely to involve a teacher in direct one-to-one teaching with a child.

A second cause for concern and potential source of frustration when planning how best to help children with difficulties, is our starting position. We begin with the knowledge that they have not learned from our best efforts to date. The teaching methods that worked with other children have not succeeded with the small group experiencing problems. This is why they present us with difficulties. If what we perceived to be our most effective methods have taught all but a couple of children, then they obviously have a learning difficulty. However, if we accept the assumptions behind the behavioural model we should be absolutely certain that everything possible has been done.

We can speculate on a scenario where the teacher acknowledges that some children present her with a considerable challenge and accepts the principles of the behavioural model. At the end of the day she chats to a couple of children who have not learned what she set out to teach. She tells them not to worry, the methods she chose did not work, she will go home, rethink the problem, and try to do better tomorrow. She reassures them that it is her problem, not theirs, and she will get it right eventually.

There is a distinct lack of information about tried and tested methods for teaching children with learning difficulties. Much of the recent interest in teaching children with special needs has tended to focus on the themes of integration, curriculum development and the effective utilisation of local education authority resources. So, whilst there has been frequent discussion on the most suitable forms of provision to meet children's needs, the topic of specific teaching methods has, on the whole, received far less attention.

Similarly, although books abound on many aspects of special education, its philosophy, psychology, sociology and classroom management, it is difficult to find many texts devoted to teaching methods and instructional techniques. Educational psychology has addressed itself to the subject, initially, through developing methods to teach the mentally handicapped. As far as teaching children with learning difficulties within mainstream education is concerned, considerably less is available to inform classroom practice.

The basis for our description of teaching methods is Haring and Eaton's (1978) Instructional Hierarchy (Table 5.3 in Chapter 5). It identifies five stages in children's learning, each one reflecting a higher order, more demanding level of performance to be achieved by the child.

The view of teaching mirrored in the Hierarchy, suggests that children must initially be shown how to use a skill and given practice so they can become fluent, before they are taught to generalise their knowledge. The end point in a programme of work is where children apply what they have been taught to real life situations, inside and outside the classroom. The Hierarchy thus attempts to guide a teacher's choice of teaching methods and patterns of classroom organisation so this aim can be achieved.

In this Chapter we describe briefly the five stages in the Hierarchy which serve as our framework for teaching, before introducing the suggested teaching methods for each stage. The Chapter concludes by taking a look at the specific teaching arrangements that are closely associated with Direct Instruction.

THE INSTRUCTIONAL HIERARCHY

Acquisition

During acquisition children are introduced to a task for the first time. Initially they are likely to make errors but over time will improve and should soon be performing to increasingly high accuracy levels. Teaching requires a high level of pupil–teacher interaction as specific techniques are used to teach each new skill.

Fluency

Once tasks are performed to high levels of accuracy, teaching concentrates on building fluency. Children work independently and are provided with plenty of opportunities to practice. Unfortunately, many of the activities that help increase fluency are repetitive and so are perhaps not as enjoyable and interesting as we might want. As a result children will appreciate regular feedback and rewards for their progress, to help keep their motivation high during this essential stage of learning.

The need to teach skills to high fluency levels cannot be emphasised enough. It makes all the difference between children learning or continuing to experience difficulties. In the past children with learning problems will probably not have been taught basic academic skills to sufficiently high fluency levels, accuracy alone providing the criteria for transferring from one task to the next.

Maintenance

We cannot afford the time to let children forget what they have learned and keep going back and reteaching skills. Over time we want to ensure children maintain their levels of performance without any further teaching taking place. However, we cannot wait for this to happen by chance, so this stage of the Hierarchy aims to teach children to reach this position.

At the end of the maintenance stage children should be able to complete tasks on their own, with accuracy and fluency, without receiving any help whatsoever from their teacher. Furthermore it is to be hoped that as they progress through each of these stages, they will become increasingly motivated to learn new skills for themselves. Once maintenance has been reached, it would be pleasing if they derived satisfaction, primarily, because they are enjoying learning and seeing they are making progress rather than because they are still being motivated by their teachers.

Generalisation

The first three stages of the hierarchy concentrate on *skill-getting*, generalisation and adaptation represent a change in emphasis to *skill-using*. Up until now children will only have been working on a single task. During generalisation they are presented with two or more tasks (which have both been taught separately and to the maintenance stage) and have to select the right response. To do this pupils are shown how to *discriminate* the critical features of each task, for example the signs for addition, subtraction, multiplication and division in numerical operations (this will be discussed further, later in this chapter).

A second type of generalisation activity is known as *differentiation*. Children give the same response to a task even though various aspects of it have changed. The way children are taught to generalise in Direct Instruction illustrates this process. In the examples presented to teach the concept 'over' (Figures 3.1 and 3.2 in Chapter 3) the position of the object varies from one presentation to the next. Nevertheless when asked where the object is in relation to the table, the child gives the same response and says 'over'. This is repeated for examples of 'not over'. The position of the object varies when it is 'not over' the table, but the pupil's response remains the same (i.e. when asked for the object's location the pupil replies 'not over').

The teacher takes an active role in teaching children how to generalise skills, whether it is via the process of discrimination or differentiation. Teaching periods are followed by intensive practice sessions where children are given a large number of generalisation activities to complete on their own.

Adaptation

In the final stage of the Hierarchy, children apply the skills they have been taught to a much wider environment. In the four previous stages children are presented with familiar tasks which are completed by providing the appropriate learned response. During adaptation children extend their skills and are faced with problems which are solved by making new and novel responses. No direct teaching occurs and the way children work can best be thought of as offering 'creative' solutions to set questions.

Changes occur in teacher involvement and the teaching approach in several ways as skills are taught at different stages in the Hierarchy. Teachers initially take an active role in the teaching process but gradually become facilitators, providing the appropriate environment in which a pupil's skill development can flourish. The teaching process itself becomes less structured over time. In the early stages teaching is very much teacher-directed, but becomes less so as the teaching arrangements are planned for successive stages.

This development is paralleled by the source of children's motivation. Initially it may well be that children, as a result of past difficulties and experiences, are reluctant learners. They do not find school interesting or rewarding and so have to be gently cajoled into starting work. The teacher plays a central role in capturing the children's interest and making learning meaningful. She achieves this in part by creating an environment in which children make progress and can see for themselves that they are improving.

In time though, it is hoped children derive pleasure because they are learning and find that they can do things that had previously baffled them. In short they become self motivating and find learning brings its own rewards. These trends are commented on as and when they occur in the description of teaching procedures for the Instructional Hierarchy.

TEACHING PROCEDURES FOR ACQUISITION

We can look at the teaching procedures for acquisition in three ways. There are the procedures which describe how tasks are presented. Then there are techniques which can be used to help children complete new skills. Finally procedures are specified for how to respond after the task has been completed.

Ways of Presenting the Task

Modelling (demonstration). The first procedure when teaching a new skill is to model the task for the pupil. The teacher starts by getting the child's attention, perhaps by saying, 'It's my turn, watch me, are you ready?' and then proceeds to complete the task, probably commenting on its key features as well. Introducing new tasks in this way draws children's attention to what is to be learned and is preferable to relying solely on a verbal description. Words on their own are rarely as effective as showing a child precisely what to do. Usually tasks are modelled on several occasions before moving on to the next procedure.

Leading. Children complete each step of the task at the same time as the teacher. When leading the teacher says to the pupil, 'Let's do this together, are you ready?' The teacher then starts and the pupil joins in, copying exactly what the teacher does. Teacher and pupil therefore perform the new task together.

Imitation. This is slightly different from leading. When the child imitates her teacher, the teacher performs the whole of the task first and only after it has been completed does the child have a turn. When leading, teacher and pupil perform the task together; when imitating the teacher completes it first and is then followed by the pupil.

Instructions. On many occasions teaching methods are accompanied by verbal instructions. Vocabulary and sentence structure should be within the pupil's range of competence and should be the same from one day to the next, as children can easily become confused if they are changed too often.

What may well seem like a small change in instructions will frequently lead to the nature of the task being changed quite dramatically. This can be illustrated by taking the example of teaching sight vocabulary to pupils with the aid of flash cards. Typically the flash cards are laid out in front of the pupil. The teacher points to each card in turn with the accompanying question, 'What does this word say?'. This is a recall task and the child tries to remember the name of the word. If the request is changed to 'Point to the word which says _____', the task becomes one of recognition rather than recall. In this case the actual word is given to the child, who then scans the array of words and points to the correct one. This is an easier activity than actually reading the word.

Test. During leading and imitation the pupil performs the task after first of all observing the teacher. Once the task can be completed accurately under these circumstances, the teacher will want to see whether the child can perform it on her own, following the appropriate instructions. Typically the pupil is told, 'Now it is your turn, are you ready?' An instruction is given and the child then tries to finish the activity *without any teacher assistance*.

Ways of Helping the Child to Succeed

Cues. These are usually visual features of the materials being used which help a pupil to succeed on a task. It could be a dot on a sheet of paper to indicate to a pupil where he should start writing from. Similarly an arrow might be used to remind a child of the direction of pencil movement required to form a letter during a handwriting lesson.

Prompts. There are times (during leading, imitation and possibly testing as well) when a pupil requires help from the teacher in completing a task. The help given is known as a prompt and can be physical, gestural or verbal.

Physical prompts are used frequently when teaching a motor skill such as handwriting. For example, a teacher could help a child having difficulty writing a particular letter, by placing the child's hand in the correct position to start writing the letter and then, if necessary, slowly guide the pupil's hand in forming the letter.

No physical contact is made with the pupil when using a *gestural prompt*. A teacher helps the pupil to complete a task by gesture alone, perhaps through pointing, nodding, directing gaze or making hand or arm movements.

Many of the Direct Instruction teaching procedures incorporate *verbal prompts* to guide pupils through tasks (for example the strategy presented in Tables 7.2 and 7.3 in Chapter 7). Alternatively a verbal prompt may simply take the form of a brief statement such as 'Which side do you start on?' or 'Write on the line', to a student working on tens and units addition problems.

Physical, gestural or verbal prompts can be used on their own, or in combination. They are provided by the teacher to help the pupil to complete the task successfully. Once this has been achieved they are gradually withdrawn so the pupil works with less teacher assistance.

Fading. The above strategy of withdrawing prompts, and it applies to cues as well, is known as fading. Children should not become over-reliant on their presence, as they must eventually perform tasks without any help.

Shaping. When shaping is used the teacher accepts an initial response on a task, even though it is not 100% correct and then praises small improvements in performance until it approaches the desired learning outcome. It is used most frequently to teach handwriting or language skills. For example, when teaching handwriting skills, a pupil would be praised for her first attempts at writing a new letter. She would be encouraged subsequently each time an improvement took place and her level of performance approached the teacher's criterion for mastery. Similarly if a child was experiencing difficulties in pronouncing certain words, the teacher would initially accept the pupil's best attempt and then reinforce subsequent improvements until the correct pronunciation was achieved.

Chaining. This is the name given to teaching a series of skills which are taught together in a specific temporal sequence. Each individual activity making up the chain, when performed in the correct order, contributes to a more complex task being completed. Many problem-solving strategies incorporate examples of chaining. Here a pupil learns how to string together a number of different skills which occur in a particular temporal order. In the strategy described in Chapter 7 (Tables 7.2 and 7.3) the pupil has already learned several skills,
- equation reading
- stating the equality rule
- pointing to the side you start with
- naming numerals (0–10)
- constructing sets
- counting from (0–10)
- writing numerals (0–10)

These skills when taught in the above sequence comprise the problem-solving strategy which is a more complex activity than each of the individual tasks.

On Completing the Task

Feedback. Feedback helps keep children motivated and interested in their work. It should be both positive and frequent to be most effective and highlight areas of educational progress. A particularly powerful form of feedback is to give children knowledge of results. They can see whether they are improving and appreciate which aspects of the task are being performed correctly and which have resulted in errors and need further practice. The value of Precision Teaching for children with learning difficulties is the way feedback is given daily as the number of correct and incorrect responses made per minute. Their progress is then emphasised by presenting it visually on specially designed charts.

Rewards. These play an important role in improving children's learning and can take several forms which are summarised in Table 10.1. Praise is probably the easiest and most natural type of reward which can be provided by a teacher, and for many children will be particularly effective. In our experience the vast majority of children in primary schools like their teachers and value their approval. They will perceive verbal praise as rewarding and will work hard to receive it.

Another powerful reward, but one that is possibly under-used, especially with younger children, is physical contact. Many young children enjoy a hug

Table 10.1   Categories of Rewards.

Category	Description	Example
Social	Pleasant interactions with other people.	Teacher praise, applause, the opportunity to sit with friends, show good work to friends and other teachers, touch (young children especially), hugs, smiles, a written note to parents about good progress.
Activity	An opportunity to take part in a particularly enjoyable activity.	Games, teacher reading an extra story, cleaning blackboard, free choice.
Tokens	A visual or tangible sign of success or approval. *The token has no intrinsic value of its own.*	Stars, points, ticks, badges, merit cards, certificates.
Material	Tangible, usable item. A material reward does have its own intrinsic value.	Sweets, trinkets, prizes, etc.

or pat on the back, etc. from their teacher. They help teachers to establish a positive and warm relationship with their children.

Tokens are useful as they can be given quickly and can then be exchanged for other rewards later on. Material rewards on the other hand are perhaps best reserved for those children who do not seem at all interested in school and who are not motivated by other types of rewards.

Diagnosing and correcting errors. From time to time pupils will make errors while being tested. On these occasions the teacher has to *think* and *react* quickly. The reason for the error has to be identified and immediate action taken, so that it does not happen again, since we do not want children to find themselves in the position of practising their own errors.

Errors can be the result of several factors. A pupil may not be attending to the teacher or task and so steps must be taken to increase the child's attention and on-task behaviour. Alternatively the pupil may make an incorrect response through lack of knowledge. This could arise when:

— the task is presented in a manner which directly leads to errors,
— the model provided is unclear and open to more than one interpretation,
— instructions are ambiguous and create confusion,
— cues and prompts are faded too quickly,
— feedback is not specific enough to help the pupil distinguish between correct and incorrect responses,
— rewards are not sufficiently desirable to increase the child's motivation.

A teacher has to think on her feet during the course of a lesson, quickly diagnose the source of the error and then take the appropriate steps to correct the mistake.

Carnine and Silbert (1979) describe one effective correction procedure involving five steps which can be used on an individual basis, or with groups of children (Table 10.2). After an error has occurred, the teacher starts the correction procedure by modelling the correct response. This is followed by leading and finally testing the pupil again in the manner described earlier.

Table 10.2 A Suggested Correction Procedure.

Step 1	Model
Step 2	Lead
Step 3	Test
Step 4	Alternate test
Step 5	Delayed test

The teacher can indicate each step by saying,
— 'My turn' (Model)
— 'Let's do it together' (Lead)
— 'Now it's your turn' (Test)

Following success on the test, the teacher alternates the item on which errors occurred with other items being taught. For example, where six letter sounds are being taught (*o*, *i*, *m*, *e*, *u*, and *s*) and errors occur in reading the letter 'o', the sequence for the alternate test may well be as follows

o, i, o, m, e, o, u, s, i, o, etc.

The procedure concludes with a delayed test. After the pupil has read the six sounds accurately, the teacher moves onto other tasks, but returns occasionally to the item on which errors were made (in this case the letter *o*).

This correction procedure is highly positive. The teacher does not criticise the pupil for making errors or failing to attend, but adopts a procedure which emphasises the correct way of completing the task.

TEACHING PROCEDURES FOR FLUENCY-BUILDING

Practice. Once a task can be performed accurately it needs to be practised so it can also be completed fluently. Haring (1978) has defined practice as 'the opportunity to perform a task repeatedly until the quality and fluency of performance increases to a specified level' (p. 14). The purpose of practice therefore, is to give the pupil as many opportunities as possible to perform the task.

At the acquisition stage of teaching, a high level of pupil–teacher interaction is required when students perform a task in order to monitor their responses carefully. This is not necessary for fluency-building. Pupils will already be able to complete the task accurately, and so a particular feature of providing practice during fluency building is students working independently with as few distractions as possible.

Feedback. A possible drawback of providing repeated opportunities for practice, is where children lose motivation and interest through the repetitive nature of the activities involved in developing fluency. Unfortunately, however, this stage is essential to future progress and cannot be left out just because it might not be appealing. Many children will acquire fluency very quickly and will require little time being devoted to practice activities. For those pupils who do not reach fluency so quickly, the teacher is faced with an uncomfortable dilemma: how to keep a child involved and sustain his interest during the periods of practice. This can be achieved in several ways (also see the section on rewards).

Firstly it is essential a pupil knows why a task needs to be practised. If an activity has a clear purpose which a child can appreciate, he is more likely to try and improve through practice. Secondly feedback of improvement helps sustain interest and takes the form of giving knowledge of results following a period of practice. Feedback can be based on the improvement reached on the practice items themselves and can be coupled with administering a probe. By placing the results on charts the pupil can readily see when his performance is improving, and this visual display of results is likely to sustain his motivation.

Rewards. Feedback is usually paired with rewards, the two procedures combining to sustain the child's enthusiasm for work. The most likely combination of rewards is social with token (points, stars, tokens, etc.) since they can be given immediately and so are particularly effective during fluency building.

White and Haring (1980) have indicated that feedback and rewards should be given at the end, rather than during, a practice session or probe. To provide either after each example or even a number of examples have been completed, would merely hinder the student's progress and slow him down. During practice the pupil must be given every opportunity to perform the task at speed without interruption so that sufficiently high fluency levels are reached.

TEACHING PROCEDURES FOR MAINTENANCE

Maintenance represents a change in role for the teacher from the active involvement of acquisition and fluency to the more passive position of facilitator, creating time during the school day for children to work on activities so that they reach a point where no further practice is required. It should be seen as a period where 'overlearning' can occur, a time where the pupil performs a skill to high levels of accuracy and fluency, but without being supported directly by the teacher and her use of teaching methods. Pupils should be engaged on the same type of practice tasks that were used during fluency building. However, any rewards that had been used previously are gradually withdrawn. The aim is for students to continue using a skill and derive intrinsic satisfaction, rather than being motivated by the teacher and her use of rewards. At the end of this stage pupils will be able to complete tasks with accuracy and fluency without any help at all from the teacher.

TEACHING PROCEDURES FOR GENERALISATION

The first three stages of the instructional hierarchy focus on presenting a pupil with a single task within a familiar format which requires a single type of response. However, eventually children need to use those skills in different and more complex settings than the ones they have hitherto experienced.

The generalisation stage therefore teaches pupils to select the appropriate response from a number of possible responses for a series of different tasks. For example, after being taught multiplication of any two numbers between zero and ten (e.g. $1 \times 10 = \boxed{}$, $3 \times 7 = \boxed{}$, $5 \times 9 = \boxed{}$ etc.), the pupil would be presented with sums of this type together with addition and subtraction sums. In such an example the pupil must make discriminations between the signs (probably by asking himself, 'Does the sign tell me to add, subtract or multiply'?) and then select the appropriate response.

This can be contrasted to situations where the student will employ the same response, computing multiplication sums, but the setting differs. For example he might use multiplication skills to complete tasks in the area of practical mathematics, possibly measurement or time problems. Similarly when children are taught to read, they need to learn that although a single word will have the same letters occurring in the same order, it will occur in many different contexts. Thus they will need to generalise their reading skills.

Several teaching procedures can be adopted to teach children to generalise (modelling, instructions, cues, testing, prompting, practice, feedback, rewards and a correction procedure) which represent procedures used both before and after the child completes the task. However, it is likely that suitable instructions alone will be sufficient for most pupils with perhaps the occasional prompt or use of cues. For example, in arithmetic sums the signs used to denote the four rules of number might initially appear in a heavy type setting to draw the pupil's attention to them. The cue could then be withdrawn after the discrimination task had been performed to a satisfactory standard.

In the early stages it is important that the pupil receives quick feedback on progress, so that confidence can be gained from completing tasks and making successful generalisations. Feedback can then be withdrawn as the children become better at generalising their skills.

TEACHING PROCEDURES FOR ADAPTATION

Adaptation is the least thoroughly investigated stage of the Instructional Hierarchy, and is therefore the most difficult one on which to give clear guidelines. The teacher takes very much a back seat during adaptation, there being no specific instructional procedures to follow. Her aim is to set pupils problems which involve them in applying previously learned skills.

Table 10.3 The Instructional Hierarchy and its Implications for Appropriate Teaching Procedures.

	acquisition	fluency	maintenance	generalisation	adaptation
Nature of task presented to pupil	All tasks require use of skill drawn from the same skill area (e.g. addition to 10)	All tasks require use of skill drawn from the same area	All tasks require use of skill drawn from the same skill area	Tasks require use of skills drawn from two or more skill areas	Task set which requires use of skills drawn from several skill areas
Response	Single response required	Single response required	Single response required	Two or more different responses required	Range of different responses required
Emphasis of instruction	Teaching skills through specific techniques which in general are presented prior to the task being completed	Child builds fluency through practice	Child maintains skills through practice	Pupil taught to make correct response through making appropriate discriminations and differentiations	Instructions given. Teacher acts as a facilitater
Feedback and rewards	Feedback and natural rewards	Feedback together with rewards is important to sustain interest	Rewards withdrawn	Feedback on success of performance (either correct or incorrect) is essential	Some feedback may occur and it is to be hoped pupils will derive personal satisfaction
Pupil/teacher contact time	High	Low	Low	High	Low

DIRECT INSTRUCTION TEACHING PROCEDURES

Direct Instruction makes extensive use of several methods already introduced to teach to the acquisition and fluency building stages of the Instructional Hierarchy, notably the 'model, lead, test' sequence, the correction procedure and regular use of feedback and rewards. The additional procedures described in this section have been designed to ensure that contact time between teacher and pupils is as effective as possible, and give children a chance to learn quickly so the gap in attainment levels that exists with their peers is bridged. Direct Instruction teaching methods focus on the use of small group instruction.

Small Group Instruction

During the course of a busy school day it is not always possible to give children having difficulties the amount of individual help they might need. One way of overcoming this problem is to teach children as a group rather than individually. Teaching up to seven or eight children in a group for 30 minutes a day could prove to be more effective and represent a more economical use of time, than teaching each student individually for the same period.

Teaching children in small groups is common practice in many primary schools. Classrooms are organised with desks and tables placed together so children can face and work with each other. Teachers go round helping children and monitor their progress and activities. Within this context small group work defines a particular pattern of organisation which then has implications for the type of work set.

In the way that group work typically operates, children work on activities which they complete at their own pace, and in a style that suits them. Unfortunately they may not be concentrating on set tasks the whole time they are supposed to be working. They might chat to friends or be distracted by other activities in the classroom. Such instances are part of everyday classroom teaching.

However, they highlight the distinction that has been made between *scheduled teaching time* and *academic engaged time*. The former refers to the amount of time set aside for different activities during the school day when children will be *expected* to work on specific activities. Academic engaged time on the other hand refers to how much time children *actually spend working*. It is the amount of time they are 'on task' and actively engaged in working on the set tasks. Inevitably children do not spend all the available scheduled teaching time actively engaged on work, and it is this situation which the arrangements for small group instruction were designed to overcome. When trying to accelerate children's progress, the teacher must do everything possible to ensure that scheduled teaching time does not just represent optimistic planning and timetabling, but becomes academic engaged time.

Research into academic engaged time is a growing area of study. For example, Rosenshine and Berliner (1978), reviewing several studies into the effects of engaged-time in teaching reading, found that *time spent* reading correlated higher with achievement than any other aspects of teacher–pupil interchanges.

Small group instruction in Direct Instruction aims to ensure children are actively engaged for as much of the designated teaching time as possible. The arrangements made may initially seem a little unusual, but they have been designed specifically for use with children experiencing learning difficulties. It is characterised by its seating arrangements and as we shall see later, by the pattern of interactions between teachers and children.

School Organisation

A prerequisite for this style of teaching is that the children who comprise the group are at approximately the same point on the curriculum and therefore need to be taught the same skills. This group could come from a single class or possibly from several classes. In either case the children will have to be withdrawn to a separate area within a classroom or out of the classroom altogether, to some alternative quiet part of the school. As a result a teacher is needed who is free from other duties and responsibilities and can devote 30, uninterrupted, minutes to teaching.

Seating Arrangements

When starting out on small group instruction the teacher sits in front of the children who then sit in a semi-circle around her. The success of the teaching session depends on the children being able to see, and hear the teacher, so they can actively participate for the entire lesson.

Unison Oral Responding

This is a critical feature of small group instruction. It ensures a high degree of active student involvement and gives children an opportunity to practise the skill being taught. The technique also helps teachers to monitor children's responses and identify pupils who are not performing at the desired level.

Teaching in this way also means that an important sixth step can be added to the correction procedure discussed earlier. The model, lead, test, alternate test and delayed test sequence can be preceded by a step where, following an error by one or more members of a group, the teacher can praise a pupil who has performed correctly and ask that child to model the task for the others. Using praise in this way helps maintain a positive atmosphere in the group and ensures pupils do not learn to make errors in order to gain teacher attention.

Signalling

One chaotic consequence of the type of small group instruction described here is all the children shouting out the answers to questions at different times. This unwelcome outcome can be prevented if the teacher orchestrates children's answers by signalling to them exactly when they are to respond, to ensure they do so together.

There are three key steps to an effective signal which indicate, directions to be followed, thinking time and when to respond. For example, in giving directions for an arithmetic task, the teacher might say, 'I'll say a number. If it's an odd number say 'odd'. If it's an even number say 'even'. Listen, seven. Is it odd or even?' After giving these directions the teacher would pause before giving the signal for the children to answer. The pause lasts for as long as it is thought necessary for all the children to work out the answer. The signal itself must be clearly seen or heard (or both) and be given quickly. It could be a hand movement, perhaps lowering it from an elevated position or possibly a clap of the hands, a signal having a visual and auditory presence.

Pacing

The lesson should be conducted at a rate which helps maintain student attention. If the lesson is too slow they will become bored and if it is paced too quickly some students may well experience difficulties in keeping up with their peers. Carnine (1976) found that during small group oral work, attending and correct answers were higher during a fast-rate lesson (5 seconds per task) than during the slow-rate lesson (14 seconds per task). During the fast-rate condition approximately 12 questions were asked per minute. Eighty per cent of them were answered correctly and students were only off-task for 10% of the time. Students were asked approximately five questions per minute during the slow-rate condition, only 30% of them being answered correctly with pupils being off-task about 70% of the time. These findings confirm what most teachers already appreciate, that it is important to maintain lesson momentum.

Monitoring

It will not be possible to monitor, simultaneously, every pupil's response during a unison response in a small group instruction, especially where the group comprises seven or eight students. Consequently, the teacher must systematically switch attention from pupil to pupil, possibly focusing on any pupil experiencing a particular difficulty.

Individual tests should be used from time to time, as they provide a more accurate indication of whether children are learning than can be gained when a group respond together. However, teachers should ideally only give individual tests after all the group appear to have mastered the examples presented, thereby avoiding the needless embarrassment of an individual child. Furthermore, if used too frequently individual tests could be time consuming and slow down the pace of the lesson.

We appreciate that you may feel ambivalent on first hearing about Direct Instruction teaching methods. They focus on aspects of teaching which run contrary to several current trends in British Education and may be anathema to some. However, there are a number of considerations which form the basis of a persuasive argument for their use.

They are only being suggested for one group of children, those experiencing learning difficulties. When circumstances permit, a number of children who are at approximately the same point on the curriculum and who need to be taught the same skills, can be taught as a group. This may well be a more effective and economical use of valuable teacher time than teaching the children individually.

The specific techniques of small group instruction, while familiar and necessary for the conductor of a symphony orchestra, may well appear to fit in less well into the classroom. Yet they all contribute to ensuring children are actively involved for the complete teaching period, and that they are positively engaged in their work.

It must also be remembered that this style of teaching would only comprise a small part of a child's school day. For the rest of the time they would be working in the usual way with the other children in their class. Furthermore the children invariably enjoy the Direct Instruction way of teaching. This has frequently baffled many teachers and yet the reason for this may lie in the fact that the children feel they are learning through being set work at an appropriate level of difficulty. They interact positively with their teacher and other children where a spirit of camaraderie and support develops.

Finally, there is now a growing body of research that demonstrates their effectiveness in teaching children with learning difficulties, which interested readers are strongly urged to consult.

This chapter has related specific methods of teaching children with learning difficulties to the five stages of Haring and Eaton's Instructional Hierarchy. Contrary to the expectations of many, only a small part of the teaching process requires a high level of pupil–teacher contact time. This occurs during the acquisition and to a lesser extent the generalisation stages. During the other stages children work independently as they practise and apply their newly learned skills. We concluded by focusing on Direct Instruction teaching methods which concentrate on how to maximise the effectiveness of small group instruction.

SUMMARY

The Instructional Hierarchy provides the framework for selecting teaching methods when teaching children with learning difficulties.

There are five stages in the Hierarchy,
- acquisition
- fluency
- maintenance
- generalisation
- adaptation

The Hierarchy stresses how children must initially be shown how to use a skill, before ultimately reaching a point where they can generalise and apply the skills and concepts they have learned to real life situations.

Different levels of direct, pupil-teacher interaction are required for each stage. It is highest for the acquisition and generalisation stages. Children tend to work independently during fluency, maintenance and adaptation.

The source of children's motivation changes as they progress through the Hierarchy. During acquisition and fluency, the teacher offers rewards and praise to help get the children interested. Over time, however, it is hoped children continue to work because they derive intrinsic satisfaction from learning and improving.

Direct Instruction teaching methods highlight the difference between scheduled teaching time and academic engaged time. They focus on the use of small group instruction and aim to maximise pupil-teacher contact time.

RECOMMENDED FURTHER READING

Ainscow, M. and Tweddle, D. A. (1984). *Early Learning Skills Analysis*. John Wiley, Chichester.

Becker, W. C. (1977). Teaching Reading and Language to the Disadvantaged — What we Have Learned From Field Research. *Harvard Educational Review*, **47**, 4, 518-543.

Becker, W. C., Engelmann, S., Carnine, D. W. and Rhine, W. (1981). Direct Instruction Model. *In* W. Rhine (ed) *Making Schools More Effective, New Directions From Follow Through*. Academic Press, New York.

Bull, S. L. and Solity, J. E. (1987). *Classroom Management: Principles to Practice*.
    Croom Helm, London.
Gulliford, R. (1975). *Teaching Children With Learning Difficulties*. N.F.E.R.-Nelson,
    Windsor.
Lockery, M. and Maggs, A. (1982). Direct Instruction Research in Australia: A Ten
    Year Analysis. *Educational Psychology*, **2**, 3–4, 263–287.

PART IV
Looking at Children's Progress

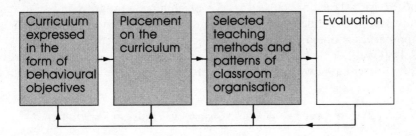

11 COLLECTING THE DATA: TASK SPECIFICATION AND PROBE DESIGN

OVERVIEW

This chapter describes:
— how probes are designed

— a quick way of describing probes

— how probes embody the characteristics of behavioural objectives

In Part IV we concentrate on the final stage of Curriculum Based Assessment, evaluating pupil progress, and in so doing discuss in some detail the principles of Precision Teaching which were introduced in Chapter 4. The two elements of Precision Teaching: collecting data on children's progress and analysing this data to make decisions about the overall effectiveness of the teaching approaches adopted, are reflected in the model described by Raybould and Solity (1982, Table 11.1). Steps 1–4 concentrate on data collection, whereas Step 5 describes how to evaluate this information and draw implications for future teaching.

Table 11.1 Five Basic Steps in Precision Teaching.

Step 1	Specify children's tasks in observable, measurable terms
Step 2	Record progress on a daily basis
Step 3	Chart progress on a daily basis
Step 4	Record the teaching approach in relation to children's progress
Step 5	Analyse the data to determine whether: — progress is satisfactory or unsatisfactory — changes are needed in teaching approach in order to maintain or accelerate progress

Chapters 11, 12 and 13 are devoted to Steps 1–3; Chapters 14 and 15 to Step 5; the fourth step, recording the teaching approach having been covered in Chapter 10. We therefore now start by looking at the relationship between specifying tasks and designing probes (Step 1).

TASK SPECIFICATION AND PROBE DESIGN

Task specification and probe design go together, hand in hand. When tasks are described in observable terms, probes can then be written to check a child's daily progress on that task. They are designed to mirror the major characteristics of the task being taught. Probes also have a particularly novel feature in that they always include more items than a child can complete in the time available.

When teaching basic literacy and numeracy skills, tasks can be drawn from three general areas which are reflected in subsequent probe design. Tasks are
— governed by a rule and contain repeated examples,
— governed by a rule but where examples are not repeated,
— not governed by a rule.

Tasks Governed by a Rule

The curricular areas where probe design is governed by rules are phonic, spelling and mathematical skills. We can illustrate how probes derived from tasks of this type are designed by looking at some examples of teaching phonic and mathematical skills.

Skill to be increased: CVCC words

bank	bend	song	mist	sink
jump	risk	left	must	wilt
hand	lisp	tent	ring	desk
bulb	gulp	left	camp	mend
link	bump	gong	left	list
hilt	band	wisp	went	wing
mask	help	bend	bank	song
mist	jump	sink	left	risk

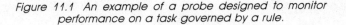

Figure 11.1 An example of a probe designed to monitor performance on a task governed by a rule.

Skill to be increased: CVCC words

skip	grab	spot	slug	stag
brim	tram	fret	scum	flag
trip	grub	snip	plug	trek
skin	stun	swot	trap	blot
plan	glum	crib	snub	drop
bled	spit	drum	slot	fret
grab	skip	slug	spot	brim
stab	fret	tram	flog	scum

Figure 11.2 An example of a probe designed to monitor performance on a task governed by a rule.

The first example to be considered is teaching children to read consonant, vowel, consonant, consonant (CVCC) words where each letter retains its own sound (e.g. lamp, test). The task is orally reading words of a particular type, and a probe can be prepared which only includes words which fall into this category (Figure 11.1). Similarly, when teaching children to read CCVC words, also where each letter retains its own sound (e.g. skip, plot etc.), a probe is designed which only includes examples representing the skill (Figure 11.2). This would therefore exclude a word such as *when*. Although the two consonants at the beginning of the word are followed by a vowel and a consonant, *when* does not represent the desired skill since the letter '*h*' is silent and does not retain its own sound. The same can be said about words like, *then*, *chip*, *shop*. The initial consonants do not retain their own sounds and are therefore governed by a different set of characteristics, which places them in another skill area (in this case consonant digraphs).

If we switch attention and now look at teaching arithmetic, a common task in the early stages is learning to add to ten (e.g. $3 + 4 = \square$). Here both addends are given and their combined total has to be worked out. A probe is

Skill to be increased: Addition to 10

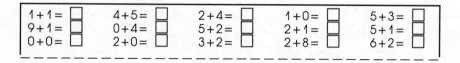

Figure 11.3 An example of a probe designed to monitor performance on a task governed by a rule.

constructed by generating many examples of addition sums of this type (Figure 11.3). No examples of subtraction, multiplication or division tasks are included, nor addition sums where the answer exceeds 10 or problems with a missing addend (e.g. $\Box + 4 = 7$ or $5 + \Box = 9$). All of these would change the nature of the task.

Tasks Governed by Rules but Where Examples are not Repeated

A second type of probe is where the items presented to the pupil occur in a sequence, governed by a set of rules, but the items themselves are not repeated. An example of such a task would be oral reading, where the order is determined, in this case, by the grammatical rules of written English. Words are sequenced systematically, rather than at random, but are not repeated. Probes of this type are frequently called *continuous* probes.

Tasks not Governed by a Rule

The third type of probe is one where examples are grouped together according to the order in which they are taught, which is determined by factors other than the distinct characteristics of the task. Teaching sight vocabulary falls into this category, since the choice of words taught is normally governed by parameters defined by the teacher, or the nature of the materials themselves:
— the student's current reading book and the new vocabulary which it introduces,
— the frequency of occurrence of words in written English.
In this curriculum area common practice is to teach pupils to read the high frequency words (e.g. and, in, it, is, an, a, here, etc.), which appear in many reading schemes and comprise a high proportion of words in written English. Teaching these words makes it easier for a pupil to transfer his reading skills from the materials on which teaching takes place, to other subject matter.

Table 11.2 Possible Word Groupings for Teaching High Frequency Sight Vocabulary.

Group 1	the a in was to
Group 2	that of and is you
Revision A	Group 1 + Group 2
Group 3	he for are it said
Revision B	Group 1 + Group2 + Group 3
Group 4	they on his with I
Revision C	Group 1 + Group 2 + Group 3 + Group 4

Skill to be increased: the a in was to
Sight vocabulary, Group 1.

the	a	in	was	to
a	the	was	to	in
to	in	was	a	the
was	to	a	the	in
in	was	to	in	the

Figure 11.4 An example of a probe designed to monitor performance on a task not governed by a rule.

The usual convention adopted to teach sight vocabulary is to include a maximum of ten words. When the total number of new words exceeds ten, then two or more probes would normally be written. Table 11.2 lists 20 high frequency words and a suggested order for teaching them based on the sequencing guidelines described in Chapter 7.

There are no specific characteristics of the words being taught which would lead to them being grouped in this way. Examples of probes not governed by a rule are shown in Figures 11.4, 11.5 and 11.6.

Skill to be increased: that of is and you
Sight vocabulary, Group 2.

that	of	is	and	you
of	is	that	you	and
and	that	you	is	of
you	and	of	that	is
is	you	and	of	that
you	and	is	of	that

Figure 11.5 An example of a probe designed to monitor performance on a task not governed by a rule.

One major consideration when teaching tasks drawn from the above three categories, is the range of generalisations that it can be predicted children can make, after being taught a skill drawn from an area governed by a rule, compared to one which is not. When tasks are governed by a rule, we can anticipate that pupils will be able to generalise from the selected examples

Skill to be increased: the a was to that of and is you
Sight vocabulary, Revision A.

that	a	in	was	to
the	of	and	is	you
a	you	to	was	that
in	the	of	and	is
was	you	of	in	and
to	is	that	a	the

*Figure 11.6 An example of a probe designed to monitor
performance on a task not governed.*

of the skill to new examples. If a child has met our criterion for reading CVCC words, we would hope the child could then read any CVCC word, including those he had not seen before.

However, such generalisations would not be possible when teaching a task where examples are *unrelated*. There is no basis on which it can be predicted that having taught a student a particular group of sight words, the pupil will then be able to read any other set of words. Learning to read a word which is one of the top ten most frequently occurring words in the English language, will not enable a pupil to read other words which also fall into this frequency band. Learning to read the words; the, was, you, etc. will therefore not necessarily help a student read any other words.

Table 11.3 summarises the relationship between probe design and curriculum area and lists some of the tasks and types of probe usually written to monitor children's progress.

Table 11.3 Common Tasks and the Type of Probe
Used to Monitor Pupil Progress.

Probe Type		
Rule	Unrelated	Continuous
Arithmetic	Sight vocabulary	Oral reading
Phonics	Spelling irregular words	Writing prose
Spelling through morphemes and sound symbol associations		

Describing Probes

White and Haring (1980) have formulated a simple way of describing probes. Their categories make it easier to specify tasks, by defining how each task is to be presented to children and the way they are to respond. The categories are:

see-to-say   — tasks are presented visually and the pupil's response is oral (e.g. oral reading of continuous prose, reading words by sight).

see-to-write   — tasks are presented visually and the pupil's response is written (e.g. writing answers to arithmetic problems).

hear-to-write — in this case tasks are presented orally and the pupil's response is written (e.g. spelling, dictation).

A common feature of Task Analysis, Direct Instruction and Precision Teaching is that all three approaches emphasise that pupils' tasks should be expressed as behavioural objectives. However, there are occasions when it can be overwhelming to write a whole series of behavioural objectives for each task on the curriculum. Tasks can often be expressed much more concisely by using the above categories. Probes embody all the features of behavioural objectives and when slotted into White and Haring's categories, make it easy to specify the nature of a task. Consider the following descriptions of a behavioural objective for teaching addition to 10 (excluding the criteria which in both examples would be 30 correct responses and a maximum of two errors per minute):

'The pupil writes answers to addition sums of the type $3 + 5 = \square$ where the answer does not exceed 10, when presented with a sheet of problems'.

This objective is equally well described by stating it is a

'see-to-write addition to 10 where the sums are of the type $3 + 5 = \square$.'

Thus, the short expressions, see-to-say, see-to-write and hear-to-write succinctly specify both the child's task and conditions for presenting the task.

The only basic skill area for which no satisfactory probing procedures have been devised, is reading comprehension. There does not seem to be a suitable way of setting criteria in comprehension based on rate measurement, which would provide a valid measure of increased proficiency in reading comprehension. However, students should still be expected to reply *accurately and fluently*, when posed graded comprehension questions following a period of oral or silent reading. We would suggest setting criteria for different comprehension skills in terms of accuracy, but also feel that the time taken to answer questions should still be taken into account.

Probes therefore reflect the nature of the task being taught which can be from one of three areas. They are described succinctly by Haring and Eaton's nomenclature and embody the characteristics of behavioural objectives. Preparing probes completes the first of the five steps involved in Raybould and Solity's model of Precision Teaching.

SUMMARY

Probes are always designed to reflect the task being taught.

Tasks are drawn from three general areas. They are:

— governed by a rule with repeated examples,

— governed by a rule but where examples are not repeated,

— not governed by a rule.

Probes always contain more items than the child can complete in the time available.

Probes can be slotted into one of three categories:

— see-to-say,

— see-to-write,

— hear-to-write.

Probes share all the characteristics of behavioural objectives.

12 COLLECTING THE DATA: RECORDING DAILY PROGRESS

```
OVERVIEW

This chapter describes:
— the characteristics of probes

— the advantages of using probes

— the information that probes give to teachers and
  pupils

— the most suitable arrangements for probing
```

Every time a child who is experiencing learning difficulties is taught, a teacher will want to know whether her teaching was effective. Were the right materials used? Were the teaching methods appropriate? Did the children learn? The more often the child is taught the greater the likelihood that a child will improve and learn. The approaches described in this book all work on this assumption and believe that it is better to teach for short periods regularly, than less frequently but for longer. Children should therefore be taught every day.

It follows that their progress should also be checked daily, to make sure they are learning. In Precision Teaching this is done through the use of probes. They enable a teacher, following each day's teaching, to monitor the child's progress and find out whether her efforts resulted in the pupil improving.

Probes serve as a 'test' but have several important characteristics, which mark them out as being quite different from any other kind of 'test' given to children. Quite naturally many teachers are concerned about the effects of frequent testing on the morale of children experiencing difficulties. Many of the tests available to teachers and psychologists, only serve to compare the progress of the child with difficulties with his more competent peers. Inevitably children become reluctant to complete these tests and the results they yield cannot always be seen as totally reliable. We cannot be sure of the children's frame of mind as they work through the tests. Are they motivated? Are they interested? Are they getting tired?

The ways in which probes differ so markedly from convential forms of testing are summarised in Table 12.1.

Table 12.1 The Special Characteristics of Probes.

They are given daily

They are given for a very short, timed period, usually one minute

Rate measurement is used as children's progress is expressed as the number of correct and incorrect responses per minute

Extremely small changes in performance can be observed

They give information on a child's level of fluency as well as accuracy

Probe results give an indication of increasing proficiency on the task being taught. The more fluent a child becomes, the greater the confidence we can have in saying the child is approaching mastery

The probe gives the teacher the chance to 'sample' the child's performance on the task being taught. Children are encouraged to work as hard as they can on the probe, which is usually for only one minute. The time periods (*referred to as record length*) are kept short to increase the liklihood of children working at an optimal level, and minimise the effects of fatigue on their performance.

Children are able to devote their full attention to the probe and are rarely distracted by other events in the classroom. A further advantage of one minute timings is that children do not become bored and give up half way through, or fail to sustain their initial enthusiasm. The longer students are asked to work on a probe, the greater the chances of this happening. On occasions when a child fails to demonstrate progress on a probe with a one minute record length, it can be tempting to increase the record length to two or three minutes' duration. However, this temptation should be resisted. In our experience Parkinson's Law operates and work expands to fill the time available. So quite often, pupils complete the same amount of work in two or three minutes as they did in one minute! The only time the record length usually exceeds one minute is during oral reading and spelling probes. The nature of these tasks makes a longer record length more suitable for sampling performance.

All the results from probes are expressed as the number of correct and incorrect responses made per minute. This means that on occasions when probes are given for longer than one minute, a standard unit of measurement is used to express the data. Rate measurement is used since it is quick, convenient and above all a consistent way of expressing progress.

Daily probing enables teachers to observe very small changes in children's performance levels, which is so important when children have failed to make progress in the past. We can illustrate the impact of this by looking at Table 12.2. This shows one child's probe data on an arithmetic task (see-to-write multiplication sums, of numbers between 0–10, multiplied by 4, e.g. $4 \times 7 = \Box$).

Table 12.2   Probe Data Collected Over a Seven-day Period Representing Small Changes in Performance.

Day	Rate Correct	Errors
Monday	10	5
Tuesday	12	5
Wednesday	18	3
Thursday	20	0
Friday	22	1
Monday	24	0
Tuesday	30	1

If we concentrate on the correct responses, the pupil made ten on the first Monday, which were increased to twelve on Tuesday. This is a small improvement, an increase of two (20%), but one which would probably have gone unnoticed without giving the probe. On Wednesday the pupil improved by 50% on Tuesday's performance! Again most teachers would be happy with any student demonstrating such progress and feel that their teaching had been extremely effective if every student improved by this amount.

This example also shows the effects of the weekend. A view frequently expressed about children with difficulties, is that they often forget over a weekend what they had learned the previous week. The probe data in the example reveals that the effects of any forgetting at the weekend were overcome by teaching on Monday, when performance levels were better than Friday's. During the seven teaching days, the child's rate of correct responses per minute trebled and the number of errors decreased from five to one.

A daily probe can give invaluable feedback to both teacher and pupil during the fluency building stage of the Instructional Hierarchy. It will prove to be an asset to the teacher in maintaining pupil motivation by demonstrating the level of progress being made each day. Teachers and children can also see how close a pupil is to approaching mastery on the task being taught.

The practical arrangements for administering probes are the same as those outlined for placement probing in Chapter 9. Time needs to be set aside so the teacher will not be interrupted while she works with an individual pupil. This means preparing work for the rest of the class which they can get on with on their own.

In our experience, the majority of teachers like to teach and then give the probe immediately afterwards. However, some teachers prefer to allow time to elapse after teaching before administering the probe. There is no right or wrong procedure here. The important principle to bear in mind is that, as far as is practicable, the teaching and probing arrangements should remain the same from day to day.

In many ways the teacher should think of herself as a scientist trying to answer the question, 'What is the most effective way of teaching this pupil?' In tackling the problem, the teacher adopts an experimental approach to teaching and after deciding what to teach, hypothesises about the most suitable setting events, selects appropriate teaching procedures and evaluates the results. When all the teaching arrangements are the same from day to day, conclusions that can be drawn about the most effective ways of teaching become more valid. Where frequent and simultaneous changes occur, for example, in the time of day of teaching, size of the teaching group, teaching procedures, etc. it becomes much more difficult to determine, exactly, which factors made significant contributions to the pupil's progress. So in deciding when to administer a probe, the important factors to remember are the time of day, the interval between teaching and probing and, finally, trying to keep this interval the same every day.

SUMMARY

Probes are given daily for short timed periods.

Probe results are expressed as the number of correct and incorrect responses per minute made by a pupil.

Use is made of rate measurement.

Probes give an indication of a child's increasing proficiency on a task.

Daily probing enables very small changes in children's performance levels to be observed.

The arrangements for teaching and probing should, as far as possible, be kept the same from day to day.

13 COLLECTING THE DATA: CHARTING DAILY PROGRESS

OVERVIEW

This chapter describes:
— the special features of the charts used in Precision Teaching

— how the charts work

— the information displayed on the charts

— the advantages of using the charts

— the information contained on a completed chart

A special type of chart is used in Precision Teaching (see Figure 13.1) called a *ratio* or *semi-logarithmic chart*. At first glance the chart may appear unfamiliar and look odd. However, it has a number of novel features which enable teachers to individualise their evaluation of children's educational progress. The charts have been specially designed to highlight the rate of children's learning, so that we can see at a glance whether they are improving quickly enough to bridge the curriculum gap.

The horizontal axis is the more common of the two, being used in many of the graphs we encounter in newspapers, on television or in children's arithmetic text books. It represents the days of the week, which are spaced at equal intervals. The distance between Monday to Tuesday; Tuesday to Wednesday; Wednesday to Thursday etc. is the same, hence this axis is described as an equal interval scale.

The vertical scale, representing the number of responses per minute, is usually the one that catches the eye, as the distance between successive numerals is not equal. The distance between 1 and 2 is greater than that between 2 and 3 which in turn is greater than that between 3 and 4. The best way of illustrating the effectiveness of this type of chart is by showing what it does.

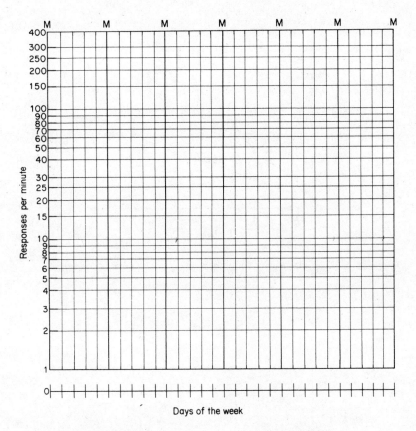

Figure 13.1 A Ratio or semi-logarithmic chart.

HOW THE CHART WORKS

Table 13.1 shows the results of two pupils, Jane and Sally who were given a daily one-minute probe for the specific task they were being taught. Both children were on the same task.

Table 13.1 Results of Jane and Sally's Daily, One-minute Probe.

	Rate correct per minute				
	M	T	W	Th	F
Jane	2	5	10	12	18
Sally	6	15	30	36	54

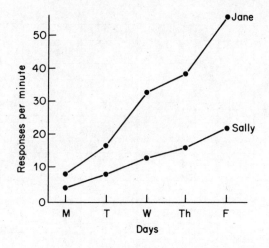

Figure 13.2   Jane and Sally's results on an interval scale chart.

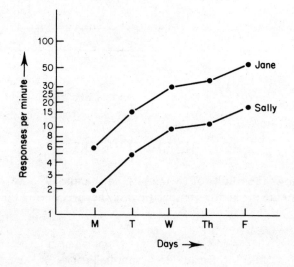

Figure 13.3   Jane and Sally's results on a ratio chart.

Figure 13.2 shows Jane and Sally's results when plotted on a conventional interval scale chart.

Looking carefully at the results on this chart would indicate that Jane is making much better progress than Sally, with higher performance levels, and it appears that the gap between the two children is widening. Now see what happens when their data is plotted on a ratio chart (Figure 13.3).

Figure 13.3 presents the results in a slightly different light. The ratio chart indicates that although Jane's absolute level of performance is higher than Sally's, their respective *rates of improvement* are the same. That is, they have both made exactly the same proportional gains in relation to their own previous perform-ance. By the end of the week, *both* children were performing at a level which was nine times better than at the beginning of the week. So although Sally is still someway behind Jane, her *rate of improvement* is the same. This effect is achieved because the vertical, logarithmic scale, shows changes of equal magnitude as an equal distance apart (2 to 4; 3 to 6; 5 to 10; 8 to 16; 20 to 40; these are all examples of improvements which are double the original performance).

Using a ratio chart might appear to be 'gimmicky' but this is definitely not the case. The ratio chart helps individualise progress by drawing attention to the pupil's progress, in relation to her own previous performance, rather than by making unfair and possibly harmful comparisons with peers. They show not only changes in absolute levels of performance but also rates of change in performance over time. Whilst ratio charts can look technical and perhaps off-putting, they have been used successfully with children of all ages. As Bates and Bates (1971) have shown, a five-year-old child can give a highly articulate account of the rationale for using this type of chart.

THE INFORMATION DISPLAYED
ON THE CHART

A closer examination of how the chart works shows that it contains two pieces of information: when information was collected, and a description of the pupil's level of performance. The horizontal axis shows when information was collected (Figure 13.4). Following each day's probing, results are recorded on the appropriate day line (a dot denoting a correct response and a cross representing errors) with a line being missed on occasions when probing does not occur.

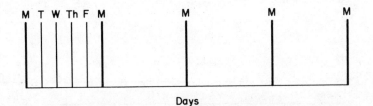

Days

Figure 13.4 The horizontal axis of a ratio chart showing when information was collected.

Generally there is no space on charts to record data on other than school days. However, some charts have been adapted to include weekend lines and are used most frequently when working with parents (White *et al.*, 1984; Solity and Reeve, 1985). Recording progress on successive calendar days has several distinct advantages. First of all, it is possible to see exactly how many days were required for a pupil to learn a particular skill. This of course includes the number of days when no teaching took place, as well as those on which teaching occurred. Secondly, it then becomes possible to compare the time taken to teach different skills. This is particularly important when decisions are taken as to whether pupils are meeting teacher expectations and learning skills quickly enough. Finally, it helps to highlight the effects of weekends, holidays, absences and other days when no teaching occurs.

The pupil's level of performance is shown on the vertical axis which is the ratio scale (see Figure 13.5). The ratio scale shows the number of responses, correct and incorrect, made per minute by the pupil on a given task. The purpose of the chart is to enable the relative (also known as proportional or ratio) gains made by the pupil to be shown (i.e. progress

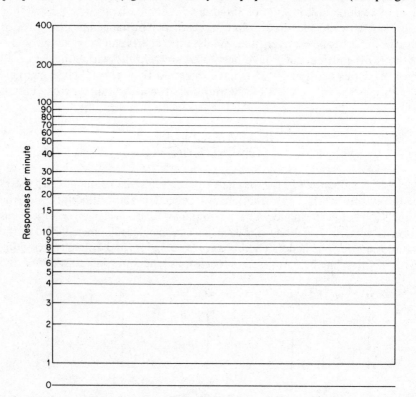

Figure 13.5 The vertical axis of a ratio chart showing the pupil's level of performance.

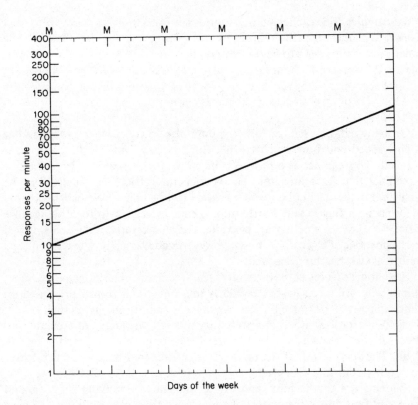

Figure 13.6 A straight line representing constant weekly progress of 50%.

from one day to the next and one week to the next), as well as the absolute performance levels reached by the pupil (i.e. number of correct and incorrect responses per minute). As a result, if a student improves by the same proportion on a weekly basis over a given period, the line drawn to represent progress will emerge as a straight line (see Figure 13.6). In the example the pupil improved by 50% (a factor of 1.5) each week and maintained this progress over a three-week period.

To summarise then, there are several advantages in using ratio charts. They clearly show small improvements that the pupil is making and give added meaning to daily probing by giving visual feedback. This will be particularly important in the early stages of teaching a skill, where efforts are concentrated on reducing the number of errors and increasing the frequency of correct responses. The more effectively that success can be demonstrated to the student the better, as this will be encouraging and motivating.

Attention is focused on the magnitude of the change (i.e. proportional or rate of progress) from day to day, rather than on the absolute improvement.

This provides the teacher with important information *in addition* to that usually available on an interval scale chart. The ratio chart also allows a wide range of academic tasks to be recorded on the same type of chart. For example, the chart can record a high rate of responses, such as might be obtained on an oral reading probe (100 or more words per minute) just as conveniently as a low rate of responses (e.g. 20 words per minute on a spelling or hear-to-write task).

Charting can be used to show the pupil the extent to which the task has been learned and how much further there is to go before the criterion is reached. This can act as a powerful incentive for pupils. It is important to remember that for many children experiencing difficulties, this will be the first time in their school careers that they will be able to see progress being made in such fine detail. Furthermore, charting can help to explain more clearly to students why they are being kept on a task, rather than being moved to the next one. They can be shown how much additional progress is required before a task has been learned.

Precision Teaching actively involves children in their teaching and learning. Pupils who are given probes regularly and have their results presented on charts quickly come to see these procedures as an integral part of their school lives. When probes are administered individually, students appreciate that the teacher is setting aside a small part of each school day to spend time with them. The very nature of the procedures ensures that this period is positive for both pupils and teachers.

Students are clearly motivated by seeing they are making progress and naturally find this immensely satisfying. Even very young children (five to six years old) can benefit from having their progress presented in this way. Although many of them will not yet have acquired the mathematical concepts to appreciate fully the numerical significance of the gains they have made, charts can still be used because of the simple concepts required to understand how progress is represented. All a pupil needs to know is:

— one line represents the number of correct responses made
— the other line represents the number of errors made
— when progress occurs the correct line will go up
— and the error line will come down

Many young children will already have learned the necessary concepts before teaching begins or, should it be required, can be taught them so they are in a position to see their learning expressed visually.

A COMPLETED SIX-WEEK CHART

Figure 13.7 shows a completed six-week chart. The student was taught on five different tasks over the six-week period. When we look at the chart we can see:

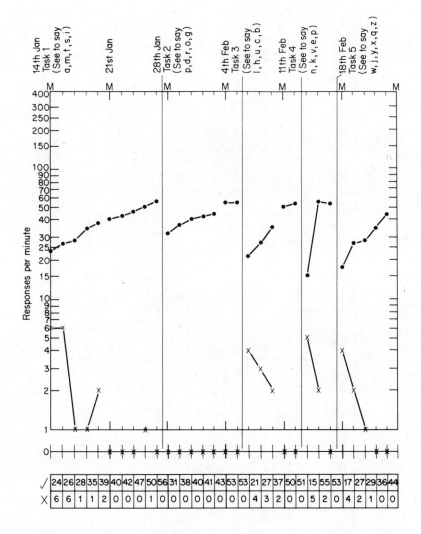

Figure 13.7   A completed chart.

Name of pupil: James   *Teacher:* Mr Smith

Task	Teaching arrangements	Data/Time	Rate		Comments
			Correct	Errors	
Task 1 see-to-say letter sounds a, m, t, s, i	Taught in a group of five children for 10 minutes. Sounds written on cards. Given opportunities to practice to increase fluency. Praised for correct answers	Wednesday 16th January 10.00 a.m.	28	1	Made progress. Increased correct responses and reduced number of errors
"	"	Thursday 17th January 10.00 a.m.	35	1	"

Figure 13.8 Plan and data sheet.

— a description of each task
— the criterion adopted for mastery on each task (50 or more correct responses per minute with a maximum of two errors on two successive days)
— the number of tasks mastered
— the number of days required to teach each task
— the dates between which each task was taught
— the effects of the weekend on performance.

Additional information is usually entered on a plan and data sheet (Figure 13.8). The first column allows the task the child is currently working on to be noted. Usually this will refer to the probe that is being used to check progress. Teaching arrangements refer to the significant aspects of the teaching environment, which help determine how effectively the child is taught. This second column will contain details of:
— duration of teaching
— specific instructions
— specific materials
— specific teaching procedures
— whether taught individually or in a group,
— amount of time allowed for practice activities.

The date and time that teaching begins is recorded. This can often be significant as it will allow observations to be made about the time of day when pupils can be taught most effectively. The results of probing are entered in column four. The final column allows space for any additional comments to be made about the pupil's progress which have not already been covered, and which it is thought will be helpful in the overall analysis of the teaching approach.

When data contained on the record sheet is coupled with that on the chart, the teacher has a considerable amount of information on what has been taught, how it has been taught and what the student has learned. All the data has been collected quickly, in a manner which can be incorporated into the context of everyday classroom practice. Equally important is the fact that the pupil has been involved in the process, by having tasks clearly specified and being given immediate feedback on progress.

The teacher has now completed Steps 1–4 of Precision Teaching and will have collected all the necessary information to begin to evaluate pupil progress. She can now analyse the data, the final and fifth step.

SUMMARY

The charts used in Precision Teaching are known as ratio or semi-logarithmic charts.

Ratio charts emphasise a child's rate of progress.

The charts display two pieces of information: when information was collected and a description of the pupil's level of performance.

The ratio chart provides the basis for evaluating progress to ensure pupils are improving quickly enough to bridge the curriculum gap.

14 MAKING SENSE OF THE DATA

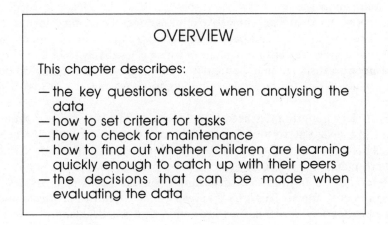

OVERVIEW

This chapter describes:

— the key questions asked when analysing the data
— how to set criteria for tasks
— how to check for maintenance
— how to find out whether children are learning quickly enough to catch up with their peers
— the decisions that can be made when evaluating the data

Analysing the data cannot happen in a vacuum. It needs to be placed in the context of the questions we want answering, the information we require to answer those questions and the criteria we bring to bear when examining the collected data. When teaching children who have experienced learning difficulties we want to know:

— whether the task has been mastered, so that a child can be moved on to the next task?
— whether the child has been learning?
— whether the child has been learning quickly enough to catch up with his peers?
— what decisions can be taken after analysing the data?

We consider each question in turn and outline the procedures developed in Precision Teaching to answer them.

HAS A TASK BEEN MASTERED?

A difficult decision facing teachers is knowing when to transfer a child from one task to another. At what point can it be said that a task has been sufficiently well taught for the pupil to be moved on to the next one in the sequence? Even experienced teachers can find this a problem.

Most teachers have their own criteria for deciding that a task has been learned, based on their experience and informal observation of the pupil's performance in the classroom. For example, a teacher would probably look to see how quickly and confidently the task was performed, how much assistance was sought when completing the task and the level of accuracy reached. Other factors might well be taken into consideration in confirming the teacher's view that the task has been learned, but essentially, these are all subjective impressions. They may change over time and for different children. It is therefore important to support such views with more objective information which is less likely to be contentious and open to dispute. It is particularly important to ensure that students who experience difficulties in learning, do not move on to a new task before they are ready.

Sufficient opportunities need to be provided to practise newly acquired tasks so they are performed fluently and maintained over time. If teaching stops before a task has been mastered it is unlikely that the student will be able to maintain previously demonstrated performance levels.

A level of fluency has to be determined for each task which ensures that this does not happen. This level is known as the *aim rate* or *proficiency level* and was described earlier as the third component of a behavioural objective, the criterion. The aim rate, once set, must *enable a pupil to maintain, or improve, her performance on a task without further direct teaching taking place.*

Setting Aim Rates

So far, when discussing aim rates or criteria in behavioural objectives (see Chapter 9), we have asked you to accept that on the tasks described, a rate of 50 correct responses, with a maximum of two errors, should be expected on see-to-say tasks and 30 correct responses with a maximum of two errors on see-to-write tasks. We now want to look briefly at the ways aim rates can be determined for individual children. Several methods are described in the literature on Precision Teaching, but the two which we have found to be most useful are those known as *previous performance* and *peer comparison*.

Previous performance. This is the method used when the pupil is being taught a series of skills sequenced, according to their level of difficulty. Under these circumstances, it is assumed that if an aim rate selected for one skill led to maintenance, it can reasonably be adopted as the aim rate when teaching the next skill in the sequence.

In the example taken from the area of phonic skills discussed earlier in Chapter 9, let us suppose that a student mastered blending CVC and CVCC words. When reading CVC words, the pupil read 64 words correctly per minute with one error and read 62 words correctly and made two errors, when reading CVCC words. The aim rate for the next skill in the sequence, reading CCVC words, could then be set at 60 or more words read correctly, with a maximum of two errors per minute.

When the first skill in a sequence is being taught and no previous data exists, an alternative approach to setting an aim rate has to be chosen. The teacher could estimate what the aim rate should be or might use the suggested aim rates in the American literature (Haughton, 1972; Formentin and Csapo, 1980). However, these rates should be seen as rough guides and only be used when no other information is available.

Peer comparison. Comparisons are frequently made between a pupil and his peers, irrespective of the teaching approaches being used. It is inevitable that those students who master a task first, will help formulate criteria in a teacher's mind, about the performance levels that need to be reached by other pupils. This principle provides the basis for determining aim rates by the method of peer comparison.

The first step is to identify a group of peers in a year or class group who have mastered the task for which an aim rate is required. A random sample of those students (approximately ten) should then be selected and given the probe for the task in question, without any teaching taking place first. The mean fluency levels for these pupils can then be calculated, and are subsequently adopted as a provisional aim rate.

The two methods outlined for setting aim rates are usually used for determining the criterion for correct responses only. It is normal practice to set the aim rate for errors, at a maximum of two errors per minute, irrespective of the task being taught.

Checking for Maintenance

Once the aim rate has been reached the pupil is transferred to the next task. At some time in the future, perhaps a week later, the probe is given again. If the rates for correct responses and errors are the same or better than a week earlier, the pupil is judged to have maintained her level of performance. On the other hand, when the student's performance deteriorates, the inference is that forgetting occurred. In such a case further teaching is required on the task. Only when performance levels are maintained on a number of occasions (weekly, monthly, termly) can it be confidently stated that mastery has occurred.

IS THE PUPIL LEARNING?

This question can be answered relatively easily, by simply inspecting the chart and asking, 'Are the child's results better today than on the previous occasions when the probe was administered?' The teacher is looking for an upward trend in correct responses and a downward one for errors. In the case of the completed chart, in Figure 13.7, the correct and error lines moved in the desired directions and progress occurred on each task. The question which still needs answering is whether progress could have been quicker: was the pupil improving at his optimal rate?

IS THE PUPIL LEARNING QUICKLY ENOUGH?

Our stated aim at the beginning of the book, is to help children with learning difficulties bridge the curriculum gap and catch up with their peers. We therefore need to know whether they are learning quickly enough to enable them to do this. Finding an answer to the question has occupied the time of many educationalists and has been tackled in a variety of ways over the years. How the question is answered depends on the expectations held about how a pupil will learn. Many, if not all, teachers hold expectations about the progress children they teach are likely to make. This is perfectly reasonable, the only problem arising when expectations are set at too high, or too low, a level and have an adverse effect on subsequent pupil performance.

Expectations about the progress children should make are shaped by a number of processes. In the past we have frequently based predictions of future progress on the results obtained from intelligence tests, the 11-plus examination being just one example of their use. It has been argued that pupils with higher intelligence levels will learn more quickly than their counterparts with lower levels of intelligence. The validity of this argument is still very much open to debate and is the subject of considerable controversy. There is not sufficient space here to discuss the use of intelligence tests as a means of forming expectations about pupil progress and interested readers are recommended to consult: Engelmann (1970); Kamin (1974); Gillie (1976, 1978); Simon (1978); Hearnshaw (1979); Beloff (1980); Eysenck and Kamin (1981).

Precision Teaching addresses itself to the problem of trying to ascertain whether a pupil is learning quickly enough. Procedures are laid down for expressing expectations and deciding how quickly pupils should learn. These place a responsibility on the teacher to collect data through systematic teaching.

Expressing Expectations

Precision teaching acknowledges that teachers hold expectations about children's progress and in keeping with the behavioural approach, requires that expectations are made explicit and revealed before teaching starts. Expectations indicate the improvement it is anticipated a pupil will make on a *weekly basis* (which also indicate expected daily progress). Once formed they are then represented on the chart, usually as a straight line. Figure 14.1 contains an example of one pupil's expected progress. Two lines have been drawn to represent the improvement a pupil is expected to make on a new task, to progress from the starting point (denoted by two small circles), to the aim rates (denoted by the symbols ∧ and ∨).

The lines are usually referred to as *minimum progress lines,* because they represent the *minimum* improvement that the pupil would have to make in order to fulfil the teacher's expectations. Note that in Figure 14.1 it was anticipated that the pupil would reduce errors and achieve high accuracy levels before concentrating on building fluency. This was indicated by showing that the aim rate for errors would be reached before the aim rate for correct responses.

Once expectations have been expressed and teaching is under way, the student's *actual* progress can be compared to the *expected* progress. When the pupil is meeting expectations, or exceeding them, correct responses will fall on or above the minimum progress line for correct responses and errors will fall on or below the minimum progress line for errors. This is shown in Figure 14.2.

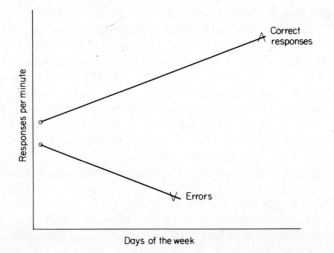

Figure 14.1 Making expectations explicit.

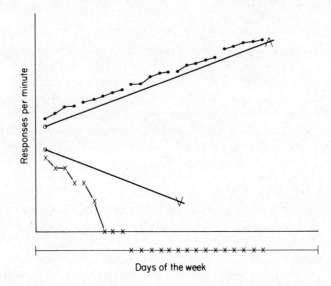

Figure 14.2 An example of a pupil meeting teacher expectations.

A final point needs emphasising here. Representing expectations for the minimum weekly improvement as a straight line might be seen as implying that progress occurs at a constant rate. This is not the case. Figure 14.3 a and b shows the progress of pupils meeting a teacher's expectations.

In both examples progress fluctuated from day to day. However, each day's correct responses were *above*, and errors below, the straight lines representing the minimum level of progress expected. The minimum progress line indicates an overall level of progress below which the pupil should not fall. Practically it is easier to express this as a straight line rather than in any other form.

Figures 14.4 and 14.5 on the other hand show patterns of responding where the pupil is not meeting teacher requirements. In Figure 14.4 although the errors fall below the minimum progress line (which is consistent with satisfactory progress) the correct responses on the final three days fell below the minimum progress line. This indicates that the rate of correct responses was not increasing in the manner anticipated by the teacher. Similarly in Figure 14.5 the errors on the last three charted days fell above the minimum progress line, again indicating that progress was not commensurate with the teacher's expectations.

It is suggested that a decision to make changes is taken when either the correct responses fall below, or the errors fall above, their respective minimum progress lines on three successive days. In both these cases the teacher would be aware that progress was not occurring at the predicted rate and would prepare to make a change in the teaching programme.

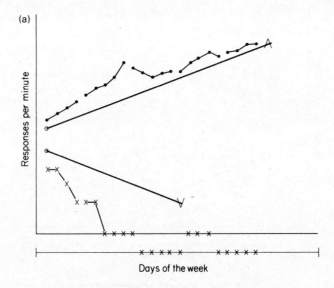

Figure 14.3a Further example of pupil meeting teacher expectations.

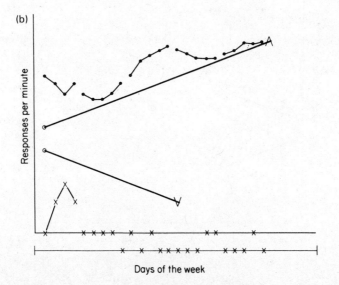

Figure 14.3b Further example of pupil meeting teacher expectations.

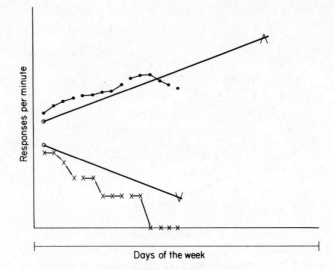

Figure 14.4 Results of a pupil failing to meet expectations as the number of correct responses fall below the minimum progress line.

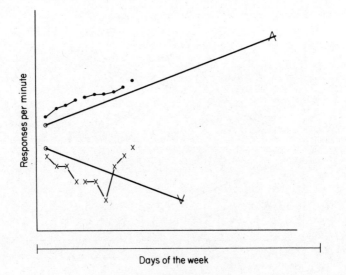

Figure 14.5 Results of a pupil failing to meet expectations as the number of errors falls above the minimum progress line.

We have described how Precision Teaching provides the means for *expressing* expectations in a way that makes them visible and perhaps more tangible, than carrying them round in our heads. How expectations are *specified* is the area to which we now briefly turn our attention.

Deciding How Quickly a Pupil Should Learn

Several procedures exist for deciding how quickly a pupil should learn, which are described in considerable detail by White and Haring (1980). Where possible this decision should be based on data that has already been collected on a pupil. One approach which does this adopts the notion of previous performance that we discussed for setting aim rates. When teaching tasks and skills drawn from a Task Analysis, the rate of progress made in learning the initial tasks in the sequence can be established. We can then predict that progress on subsequent tasks will be at a similar or quicker rate.

An alternative approach is used in the absence of any other data. In this case, the teacher specifies a standard weekly improvement that a pupil ought to make. A teacher might feel that until other information becomes available, weekly gains in excess of 50% are desirable and the minimum progress line is then set to represent this rate of progress. Such a decision is inevitably somewhat arbitrary but is an acceptable short-term measure. At the very least, it gives the teacher a yardstick by which she could judge whether or not satisfactory progress is being made.

Finally, a teacher could base expectations of pupil progress on the number of tasks to be taught during the academic year, for a given curriculum area, so that a child can bridge the gap with his peers. It might emerge that 20 tasks have to be taught over a 40-week period, meaning that each one must be learned within a fortnight. The minimum progress lines would therefore be set to reflect this.

WHAT DECISIONS CAN BE TAKEN
WHEN ANALYSING THE DATA?

Setting aim rates and minimum progress lines provides the context for evaluating children's progress. The purpose of analysing charted data is to determine whether the pupil's progress meets the specified expectations. Where it does, the pupil is regarded as *keeping on course for success*, but if on the other hand it does not, changes have to be made in the teaching approach. Four questions can be asked when evaluating a child's learning outcomes and comparing recorded progress with expected progress.

Has the Aim Rate Been Reached?

If so the pupil is transferred to the next task.

Is Progress Towards the Aim Rate Satisfactory?

Yes, as long as the correct responses are on, or above, the minimum progress line and errors are on, or below, the minimum progress line. Carry on teaching the same skill with the same teaching arrangements (unless the purpose of instruction changes from establishing accuracy to building fluency). Sometimes, however, either the correct responses fall below the minimum progress line, or the errors are above the minimum progress line, *but only for one or two days*. When this happens, teaching is still regarded as satisfactory and continues with no adjustments being made to either the skill taught or teaching approach. It is too early to make any changes after two days, the lack of progress being attributed to chance factors such as either the pupil or teacher having an 'off day'.

Is Progress Towards the Aim Rate Unsatisfactory?

Yes, when expectations are not being met on three successive days (as illustrated in Figures 14.4 and 14.5). As a result a change is made in the programme so the maximum period of time where teaching is regarded as unsuccessful is three days, after which ameliorative action is taken.

Were My Original Expectations Realistic?

Setting expectations for pupil progress is not a clear-cut, definitive process. Errors can and invariably are made. The dangers of setting expectations at too low a level have been well documented in recent years (Rosenthal and Jacobson, 1968; Pidgeon, 1970; Elashoff and Snow, 1971; Hargreaves, 1972; Brophy and Good, 1974; Insel and Jacobsen, 1975; Burns, 1982). Equally they might be set at too high a level and this possibility must always be explored when children do not progress in the way we originally hoped. There are times when, in the light of the available data, expectations will have to be revised and reset at more realistic levels.

It must be remembered that teaching is only described as successful or unsuccessful *in relation to the teacher's expectations*, as represented by the minimum progress lines and not solely on the basis of the frequency of correct and incorrect responses. It is therefore conceivable that a pupil's performance could improve daily, in the sense that the number of correct responses per minute increased and the number of errors decreased, but is viewed as unsatisfactory because the proportional gains occurring from one day to the next were not as large as expected. This is illustrated in Figure 14.6.

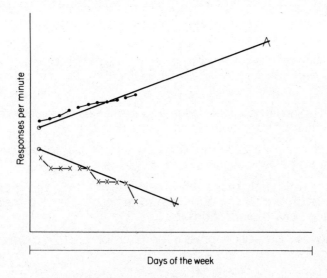

Figure 14.6   A pupil failing to meet expectations even though the number of correct responses increased and the number of errors decreased from day to day.

Progress was made, the number of correct responses continued to increase (and the number of errors decreased over the final three days' tuition) but was, nevertheless, not happening as rapidly as the teacher predicted.

In this chapter we have explained the reasons for making our expectations explicit. The methods outlined for doing this are guidelines only, rather than hard and fast rules. They will help to make the process overt and therefore clear for all to see.

As far as possible expectations should be based on data that has been collected in the classroom. They are presented on the ratio charts as straight lines which are known as minimum progress lines. Expectations are set at a level which reflects the rate of progress a child needs to make in order to bridge the gap in attainment levels that exists with her peers.

SUMMARY

The aim rate must enable pupils to maintain or improve their performance on a task without further direct teaching taking place.

The two methods used for setting aim rates are known as *previous performance* and *peer comparison*.

Procedures are laid down for expressing expectations and deciding how quickly pupils should learn.

Minimum progress lines represent the minimum improvement that a pupil has to make in order to meet a teacher's expectations.

Children's actual progress is then compared to expected progress.

Four questions can be asked when evaluating children's progress:
  — has the aim rate been reached?
  — is progress towards the aim rate satisfactory?
  — is progress towards the aim rate unsatisfactory?
  — where my original expectations realistic?

Teaching is only described as successful or unsuccessful in relation to a teacher's expectations as represented by the minimum progress lines.

15 GETTING BACK ON COURSE FOR SUCCESS: MAKING PROGRAMME CHANGES

OVERVIEW

This chapter describes:
— four ways of making changes to the programme

— how changes for different stages in the Instructional Hierarchy relate to the sequence; setting events, behaviour and consequences (described in Chapter 1)

— how to make provision for children with physical difficulties

When children are not making the necessary progress to catch up with their peers in learning basic academic skills, changes need to be made in the teaching programme. Any changes should be introduced systematically, with only one amendment taking place at a time. Its impact can then be observed, so that ultimately, effective changes can be recorded and noted. When two or more changes are implemented simultaneously, which result in an increased rate of learning, the teacher would be unsure of which change led to the improvement.

There are four ways of making changes to the programme.

CHANGE THE SEQUENCE OF TASKS OR SKILLS

We have stressed the need, throughout the book, to have a well planned curriculum and to place children accurately on that curriculum. In the early days of implementing a new curriculum a teacher has to ask himself whether skills have been sequenced appropriately. The sequencing guidelines presented in Chapter 7 can help in double-checking that this is so. However, where a teacher experiences considerable difficulties in teaching a particular skill to a large number of children, the skill may well be misplaced on the curriculum.

Alternatively, although the sequence of skills could be acceptable, the actual step size between skills might be too great. Further analysis of the curriculum may well indicate that an important skill had been omitted during the original Task Analysis which caused the subsequent difficulties.

Finally, a look at a pupil's pattern of errors could reveal that his performance on an earlier skill had for some reason not been maintained. Under these circumstances, it is necessary to go back and provide further teaching on that skill.

CHANGE TASK OR SKILL SLICES

Once it has been confirmed that the skill being taught is the appropriate one for the pupil, it might be that the demands of the task or skill will need to be reduced by continuing the analysis. This subject was first introduced in Chapters 2 and 6 where we indicated that there are numerous ways in which any given task and skill can be made easier. It is possible that the source of the difficulties lies in the way the task and skill slices have been identified. For example, if one series of slices was initially unsuccessful, alternatives would need to be tried. The range of feasible slices can be illustrated if we look at teaching children to read consonant, vowel, consonant, (CVC) words where the medial vowels are *a*, *e*, *i*, *o*, or *u*. There are several ways in which this skill can be made less demanding for a pupil. Figure 15.1 shows how it can be simplified by grouping CVC words by their medial vowel and teaching words with the same medial vowel together. All the CaC words would be taught first, followed by CeC, CiC, CoC and finally CuC words.

The skill can be broken down even further and thus made easier by then teaching CVC words which start with a continuous sound (a sound that can be held e.g. *f*, *l*, *m*, *n*, *r*, *s*, *v*, *w*, *z*) before those beginning with a stop sound (sounds which cannot be held e.g. *b*, *c*, *d*, *g*, *h*, *j*, *k*, *p*, *q*, *t*, *x*, *y*). Carnine and Silbert (1979) have suggested it is easier to teach CVC words beginning with a continuous sound than those beginning with a stop sound. All told, there are 15 possible slices when teaching CVC words. No doubt, alternative slices could also be identified.

CHANGE THE TEACHING APPROACH

There are three areas where the teaching approach can be changed: organisational features of the classroom, teaching arrangements and teaching

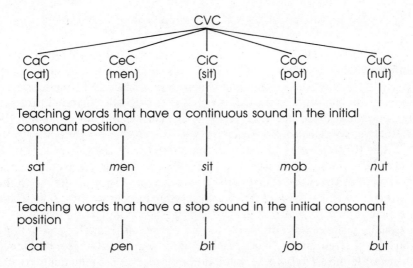

Figure 15.1 *Range of possible slices for teaching CVC words.*

procedures. Programme changes of this type relate back to the original selection of teaching methods discussed in Chapter 10, or refer to some of the wider aspects of classroom management described in detail in Bull and Solity (1987). When changing the teaching approach, changes are usually made to improve rate of acquisition and often focus on the choice of teaching procedures, in particular, ways of presenting the task (modelling, leading, imitation, instructions) and ways of helping the child to succeed (cues, prompts, shaping, chaining).

For example, the teacher might need to model completion of the task more often; provide further opportunities for the pupil to imitate the teacher; change the instructions; alter the nature of cues and prompts and during fluency-building, children may be given additional examples on which to practise. Only one change should be made at a time, it can then be recorded on the plan and data sheet with its effects on pupil progress being observed and evaluated.

Amendments to teaching procedures can therefore be seen as falling into the following areas:
— increase the help provided (e.g. cues *plus* prompts),
— change from one teaching procedure to another (e.g. from using cues to prompts),
— modify an existing procedure (e.g. alter the instructions),
— increase or decrease the frequency with which a procedure is used (e.g. increase the frequency with which the teacher models the task for the pupil),
— increase or decrease the period of time the pupil practises a new skill,
— change the teaching materials.

INCREASE MOTIVATION

When teaching a skill it is to be hoped that pupil motivation will remain high. Unfortunately this will not always be the case and there will be times, most frequently during fluency-building, when changes need to be made to help improve motivation. Consequences which were originally found reinforcing by a pupil may no longer be effective, so the teacher will have to search for alternatives to increase motivation.

Within the framework of the Behavioural Model and the sequence: 'setting events, behaviour, and consequences', Haring *et al.* (1981) have outlined the most suitable times for selecting the above changes. They are linked to the Instructional Hierarchy and the stage reached in teaching a given skill. These are summarised in Table 15.1.

Usually changes are only made during the acquisition, fluency-building and generalisation stages. When teaching at the acquisition stage, programme changes are most likely to be made in the setting events (changing aspects

Table 15.1 Relationship Between Programme Changes, the Instructional Hierarchy and the Sequence: Setting Events, Behaviour and Consequences.

	Setting events	Behaviour	Consequences
Acquisition	Change the sequence of tasks or skills Change the sequence of slices Change the organisational features of the classroom Change ways of presenting the task	Change ways of helping the child to succeed	
Fluency-building		Provide increased opportunities for practice	Increase motivation
Generalisation	Change the instructions to the pupil	Change ways of helping the child to succeed	Change the way feedback is given Increase motivation

of the task), or the pupil's behaviour (changing the ways of helping the child to succeed). During fluency-building changes centre on providing increased opportunities for practice or the consequences of successfully completing a task (altering the rewards). When teaching generalisation skills, aspects of setting events (instructions), the pupils' behaviour (ways of helping children succeed) or the consequences (changing the nature of feedback or increasing motivation) can be changed.

ACCOUNTING FOR PUPILS WITH PHYSICAL DIFFICULTIES

An important area which needs to be considered in relation to Precision Teaching is the impact of a pupil's physical skills on his mastery of basic academic tasks. The name given to the physical side of a task is *tool skill rate*. It is the time a child takes to perform the physical requirements of a task and excludes 'thinking time'. During a one-minute probe, part of the minute is spent selecting the appropriate response. This is the thinking time. The rest of the minute involves communicating the answer in one of several forms (i.e. oral, written, drawn, etc.). It is the time spent *making* the response that is known as the tool skill rate.

These relationships can be expressed in an equation:

Time taken to = Time taken to arrive + Time taken to
complete the   at the correct   complete the physical
task   response (i.e.   requirements of the
                 thinking time)   task (tool skill rate)

When probes are given to a student it is usually assumed the pupil has the necessary physical skills to complete the task. Unfortunately this is not always the case. There are occasions when a student fails to make the desired progress, not because the teaching of that skill has been ineffective, but because the pupil does not have the physical skills necessary to respond quickly enough to the task. This assumption is most often seriously tested in the area of arithmetic, where experience has revealed the existence of large discrepancies in children's tool skill rates for writing either single, double or treble digits (e.g. Vaughan, 1982; Wiehl, 1982). As a result it is often important to bear in mind that there might be occasions when a pupil has difficulty reaching a specified aim rate because of physical difficulties.

For example, consider the pupil working on subtracting numbers between 0–10 from 10, where the aim rate was set at 25 correct responses per minute with no more than two errors. What if it transpired that the pupil's tool skill rate for the task did not exceed 15 responses per minute? In other words, even when no thinking was required the pupil could not provide more than 15 responses in the minute. It would therefore be unrealistic to expect the pupil to achieve an aim rate of 25 correct responses which included thinking time as well. In such instances time has to be spent helping the student increase his speed in writing numerals before continuing instruction in subtraction skills.

To summarise therefore, minimum progress lines (described in Chapter 14), enable teachers to make their expectations for pupil progress explicit. Should children's actual progress fail to meet these expectations, changes are made in the teaching programme to put them *back on course for success*.

SUMMARY

There are four ways of changing the programme:
— changing the sequence of tasks or skills,
— changing the task or skill slices,
— changing the teaching approach,
— increasing pupil motivation.

Programme changes occur most frequently during the acquisition, fluency-building and generalisation stages of the Instructional Hierarchy.

These changes are related to the sequence: setting events, behaviour and consequences.

Tool skill rate is the time a pupil takes to complete the physical requirements of a task and excludes thinking time.

PART V
Conclusion

16 OVERVIEW

Recent years have seen a steady increase in the use of behavioural approaches to teach children with special needs. In this book we have concentrated on three approaches; Task Analysis, Direct Instruction and Precision Teaching and discussed their contributions within the framework of Curriculum Based Assessment (CBA).

CBA highlights four areas: curriculum design, placement on the curriculum, selecting teaching methods and evaluating progress, which provide the basis for assessing children's educational needs. Assessment within this context is seen as a continuous process, something that happens daily and *which is closely related to teaching*.

Task Analysis, Direct Instruction and Precision Teaching are involved at different stages during the process, emphasising different principles and aspects of effective teaching. They are three highly complementary approaches, sharing similar assumptions and hopes for children experiencing learning difficulties; namely that they will be able to bridge the gap in attainment levels that exists with their peers. This will arise through their academic progress being accelerated and systematically evaluated so that, as far as possible, they are being taught by the most effective methods available.

In this overview we will summarise the contributions of each approach in the process of CBA.

DESIGNING THE CURRICULUM

The Task Analytic Model is a seven-step procedure for designing the curriculum. Tasks are analysed into sequences of skills, which are then arranged and taught according to their level of difficulty. However, if children are to catch up with their peers, and if they do not automatically generalise the skills they have learned on their own, they must be taught how to do so. This aspect of teaching is emphasised in Direct Instruction and achieved through preparing problem-solving strategies. The strategies link similar skills and mean that they can be taught together rather than being isolated and tackled separately. Once children have learned the necessary strategies they will be in a position to generalise their newly acquired skills.

The principles of Task Analysis and Direct Instruction also offer an invaluable basis from which to evaluate and adapt existing published materials. These materials, although often suitable for the majority of children in a class, are not always able to meet the requirements of the child experiencing difficulties. There are a number of reasons for this: the sequence of skills may not be appropriate; tasks might not be clearly specified; they may not provide sufficient practice items; instructions to the teacher or those for the teacher to give the child could be ambiguous, etc. As a result the published materials would need to be amended so they can still help the teacher fulfil her aim of accelerating children's progress.

PLACEMENT ON THE CURRICULUM

Placement probes developed from the principles of Precision Teaching provide an effective way of placing children accurately on the curriculum. It is clearly important that the skills children are taught must be at just the right level of difficulty. When they are not and especially if they are too hard, both teacher and child can become frustrated and disappointed and ultimately feel like giving up.

An appealing feature of placement probes is that they are designed to mirror the curriculum being used by an individual school and are therefore sensitive to the tasks children are currently being taught. The probes themselves can be given quickly, each one usually taking no longer than one minute and they tell the teacher exactly which skills have been learned and which ones need to be taught next.

DECIDING HOW TO TEACH

Haring and Eaton's (1978) Instructional Hierarchy outlines five levels of teaching which reflect how children learn new skills. The principles embodied by the Hierarchy emphasise just why teaching to high levels of accuracy and fluency is so important. It is felt that if children cannot use skills fluently, they will soon be forgotten and valuable teaching time will have been wasted. High fluency levels are the springboard from which children are able to continue using skills even after any direct teaching has been withdrawn, and from which they are subsequently shown how to generalise and apply their knowledge.

Each level in the Hierarchy is closely associated with specific teaching methods which have been developed through the application of behavioural principles to teaching. These are augmented by the methods favoured within Direct Instruction for organising effective small group instruction. Some aspects of small group instruction are unfamiliar within most educational setting within the United Kingdom and it would be true to say have been viewed with suspicion at times. Yet they have a clear rationale and purpose. Their role is to enable a teacher with a limited amount of time, but a number of children at approximately the same place on the curriculum, to teach those children together. As you will appreciate this could quickly become disorganised and chaotic unless the teacher has a clear set of procedures to follow. Finally, it must be remembered that academic engaged time is high for all children.

EVALUATING CHILDREN'S PROGRESS

Children's progress is evaluated through the techniques derived from Precision Teaching. Daily probes give feedback on just how quickly they are learning, whilst at the same time letting the teacher know which teaching methods and patterns of classroom organisation are being most effective. As a result of checking progress every day we can make sure children are learning, and learning at a rate which we consider to be quick enough to enable them to bridge the gap in skill levels that exists with their peers.

Precision Teaching offers the means to answer the key questions which are so important when trying to accelerate children's progress. We are in a position to find out whether children are on the right task, whether they are learning quickly enough to catch up with their peers and whether they have learned the task they have been working on. By establishing criteria based on fluency levels for every task taught, teachers, children and parents alike can all see what level of performance has to be achieved to show that a new skill has been learned.

The purpose of this book has been to describe the assumptions, aims and techniques of three approaches to teaching children with learning difficulties, based on the principles of behavioural psychology. We felt there was a need to illustrate how the approaches interrelate and offer a positive basis on which to plan and implement teaching.

The behavioural approach to teaching concentrates on factors within a teacher's sphere of influence in the classroom and those are what we have focused on in this text. We do not believe that there is any one way of teaching which meets the needs of all children. They learn through a variety of means, some of which we are aware and others of which we are not. The appeal to us of the approaches we have described is the sense of optimism they convey about children experiencing difficulties. They say children can and will learn if we get the teaching right. Furthermore they give the classroom practitioner clear guidelines about exactly how to go about teaching.

Translating principles to practice will require considerable commitment and much effort. However, when children *bridge the curriculum gap* the rewards for all concerned, parents, teachers and children, will make it worthwhile.

BIBLIOGRAPHY

Barker-Lunn, J. C. (1970). *Streaming in the Primary School.* National Foundation for Educational Research, Windsor.

Bates, S. and Bates, D. F. (1971). ". . . and a Child Shall Lead Them": Stephanie's Chart Story. *Teaching Exceptional Children*, 3, 111–113.

Beloff, H. (1980). A Balance Sheet on Burt. *Supplement to the Bulletin of the British Psychological Society*, 33.

Bereiter, C. and Engelmann, S. (1966). *Teaching Disadvantaged Children in the Preschool.* Prentice Hall, New Jersey.

Blankenship, C. and Lilley, M. S. (1981). *Mainstreaming Students with Learning and Behaviour Problems.* Holt, Rinehart and Winston, New York.

Brophy, J. E. (1974). *Teacher-Student Relationships.* Holt, Rinehart and Winston, New York.

Brophy, J. E. and Good, T. L. (1974). *Student–Teacher Relationships.* Holt, Rinehart and Winston, New York.

Burns, R. (1982). *Self-Concept Development and Education.* Holt, Rinehart and Winston, London.

Bull, S. L. and Solity, J. E. (1987). *Classroom Management: Principles to Practice.* Croom Helm, London.

Carnine, D. W. (1976). Correction Effects on Academic Performance During Small Group Instruction. *In* W. C. Becker and S. Engelmann (eds) *Technical Report 1976–1 Appendix B: Formative Research Studies.* University of Oregon, Eugene.

Carnine, D. W. and Silbert, J. (1979). *Direct Instruction Reading.* Charles E. Merrill, Ohio.

Department of Education and Science (1978). *Special Educational Needs* (The Warnock Report). H.M.S.O., London.

Department of Education and Science (1981). *Education Act.* H.M.S.O., London.

Department of Education and Science (1983). *Assessment and Statements of Special Educational Needs.* Circular 1/83.

Elashoff, J. and Snow, R. E. (1971). *Pygmalion Reconsidered.* Jones, Ohio.

Engelmann, S. (1970). The Effectiveness of Direct Instruction on I.Q. Performance and Achievement in Reading and Arithmetic. *In* J. Hellmuth (ed) *The Disadvantaged Child* (Vol 3), pp. 339–361. Bruner-Mazel, New York.

Engelmann, S. and Carnine, D. W. (1982). *Theory of Instruction: Principles and Practice.* Irvington, New York.

Eysenck, H. J. and Kamin, L. (1981). *Intelligence: The Battle for the Mind.* Pan, London.

Formentin, T. and Csapo, M. (1980). *Precision Teaching.* Center for Human Development and Research, Vancouver, Canada.

Gillie, O. (1976). Crucial Data was Faked by Eminent Psychologist. *Sunday Times*, 24th October.

Gillie, O. (1978). Sir Cyril Burt and the Great I.Q. Fraud. *New Statesman*, 24th November.

Glaser, R. (1962). *Training Research and Education.* University of Pittsburg Press, Pittsburg.

Gronlund, N. E. (1970). *Stating Behavioural Objectives for Classroom Instruction.* Macmillan, New York.

Haring, N. G. and Eaton, M. D. (1978). Systematic Instructional Procedures: An

Instructional Hierarchy. In N. G. Haring *et al.* (eds), *The Fourth R—Research in the Classroom*, pp. 23–40. Charles E. Merrill, Ohio.

Haring, N. G., Liberty, K. A. and White, O. R. (1981). *An Investigation of Phases of Learning and Facilitating Instructional Events for the Severely/Profoundly Handicapped*, Final Project Report (Project No. 443CH70564). University of Washington, Seattle.

Hargreaves, D. H. (1972). *Interpreting Relations and Education*. Routledge, London.

Haughton, E. (1972). Growing and Sharing. *In* J. B. Jordan and L. S. Robbins (eds) *Let's Try Doing Something Else Kind of Thing*, pp. 20–39. The Council for Exceptional Children, Arlington, Virginia.

Hearnshaw, L. S. (1979). *Cyril Burt: Psychologist*. Hodder and Stoughton, London.

Howell, K. W., Kaplan, J. S. and O'Connell, C. Y. (1979). *Evaluating Exceptional Children: A Task Analytic Approach*. Charles E. Merrill, Columbus, Ohio.

Howell, A., Walker, R. and Fletcher, H. (1981). *Mathematics for Schools*. Addison-Wesley, London.

Insel, P. and Jacobson, L. (1975). *What Do You Expect?* Cummings, Menlo Park, California.

Junkula, J. (1972). Task Analysis and Instructional Alternatives. *Academic Therapy*, **8**, 33–40.

Kamin, L. J. (1974). *The Science and Politics of I.Q.* Wiley, New York.

Mager, R. F. (1962). *Preparing Instructional Objectives*. Fearson Publishers, Belmont, California.

Pearson, L. and Tweddle, D. A. (1984). The Formulation and Use of Behavioural Objectives. *In* D. Fontana (ed) *Behaviourism and Learning Theory in Education*, pp. 75–92. British Journal of Educational Psychology Monograph Series No. 1, Scottish Academic Press.

Pidgeon, D. A. (1970). *Expectation and Pupil Performance*. N.F.E.R., London.

Raybould, E. C. (1984). Precision Teaching and Pupils with Learning Difficulties— Perspectives, Principles and Practice. *In* D. Fontana (ed) *Behaviourism and Learning Theory in Education*, pp. 43–74. British Journal of Educational Psychology Monograph Series No. 1, Scottish Academic Press.

Raybould, E. C. and Solity, J. E. (1982). Teaching with Precision. *Special Needs/Forward Trends*, **9**, 2, 9–13.

Rosenshine, B. V. and Berliner, D. C. (1978) Academic Engaged Time. *British Journal of Teacher Education*, **4**, 3–16.

Rosenthal, R. and Jacobson, L. (1968). *Pygmalion in the Classroom*. Holt, Rinehart and Winston, New York.

Silbert, J., Carnine, D. W. and Stein, M. (1981). *Direct Instruction Mathematics*. Charles E. Merrill, Ohio.

Simon, B. (1978). *Intelligence, Psychology and Education*. Lawrence and Wishart, London.

Solity, J. E. and Reeve, C. J. (1985). Parent Assisted Instruction in Reading and Spelling (P.A.I.R.S.). *In* K. Topping and S. Wolfendale (eds) *Parental Involvement in Children's Reading*. Croom Helm, London.

Southgate, V., Arnold, H. and Johnson, S. (1981). *Extending Beginning Reading*. Heinemann, London.

Tomlinson, S. (1982). *A Sociology of Special Education*. Routledge and Kegan Paul, London.

Vargas, J. S. (1977). *Behavioural Psychology for Teachers*. Harper and Row, New York.

Vaughan, M. J. (1982). A Study of the Relationship Between Performance Standards Attained in Mathematical Skills and the Efficiency with which they are Maintained. M. Ed. Dissertation, University of Birmingham. Unpublished.

White, O. R. (1981). *Making Daily Classroom Decisions*. Paper Presented at the National Conference of the American Educational Research Association, Los Angeles, California.

White, O. R. and Haring, N. G. (1980). *Exceptional Teaching*. Charles E. Merrill, Ohio.

White, P. G., Solity, J. E. and Reeve, C. J. (1984). Teaching Parents to Teach Reading. *Special Education/Forward Trends*, **11**, 11–13.

Wiehl, P. D. (1982). A Pilot Study in Parental Involvement with Junior School Children in the Learning of Early Number Skills. M. Ed. Dissertation, University of Birmingham. Unpublished.

Ysseldyke, J. E. and Salvia, J. (1974). Diagnostic-Prescriptive Teaching: Two Models. *Exceptional Teaching*, 181–186.

INDEX

teaching procedures, 54, 67
  (*see also* deciding how to teach:
      direct instruction teaching
      procedures; teaching
      approach)

test, 83, 89
tool skill rate, 137–8

Warnock Report, 35